MINGJUE AWAKENING

Teachings on Pure Consciousness
Collective Field Qigong and Energy Healing

Wei Qifeng

Based on Zhineng Qigong Theory and Methods
by Dr. Pang Ming

Edited by Cynthia Li, MD

Cultivating qi
is not the most fundamental;
cultivating one's spirit is.
Mastery of qi
is really achieved
through mastery of consciousness.

Dr. Pang Ming, founder of Zhineng Qigong

A BLESSING FROM TEACHER WEI

My wish is for everyone to have a harmonious and centered consciousness state, to continue developing this state, and to enjoy life in this conscious entirety (oneness) state.

May we not be attached to and limited by external things, which can create suffering. Instead, may we each go deep within ourselves, remaining there with increasing stability. This can make our collective essence and presence brighter and stronger. By helping our inner selves grow, we also help the whole world.

Pure Consciousness and the consciousness field are like this. When we connect with them, it doesn't mean we attach to them. It means we go deep inside both ourselves and the collective field and stay in the purest state. The field supports us with good information and universal love.

In truth, we are the consciousness field. The collective consciousness field is around us but also within us. When we come to Mingjue (Pure Consciousness), there is no separation between the collective field and the consciousness of self. There is also no difference between Mingjue and the universe.

I wish everyone happiness, from heart to heart. Life in this conscious entirety is beautiful!

Hùn Yuán Líng Tōng

Wei Qifeng
June 2023

photo: An Yua

ABOUT TEACHER WEI

Wei Qifeng is a master teacher and healer in the lineage of Zhineng Qigong. He completed the two-year masters training program under the founder of Zhineng Qigong, Dr. Pang Ming, at the Huaxia Zhineng Qigong Center – "Medicineless Hospital" – in China from 1993-1995. Subsequently, he served at the center as a healer, editor, and lead teacher to some 500-600 hospital staff in morning and evening practices.

Since 2006, he has been highlighting the development of the Pure Consciousness state – or Mingjue – as his foundational teaching, with the qigong movements guided from this expanded mindset to amplify healing and awakening. This highest level of practice, he says, from a collective field in which practitioners connect in Pure Consciousness, has the greatest potential for deep transformation, personal and global.

In 2018, Teacher Wei co-founded The World Consciousness Community to build a worldwide consciousness field, "to connect practitioners heart to heart in the Mingjue state, to support each other and to enhance a higher consciousness for peace, freedom, healing, love, happiness, and harmony for each individual as well as the whole world." He is the founder and organizer of Harmonious Big Family, Dao Hearts, and the Mingjue Academy.

He has also translated several of Dr. Pang's books into English.

ABOUT THE EDITOR

Cynthia Li, MD, is an American medical doctor and author. Her personal journey through a complex autoimmune condition took her from public health in underserved communities to integrative medicine and intuitive healing, and was featured in Kelly Turner's acclaimed documentary, *Radical Remission*.

Dr. Li has studied with functional medicine experts, environmental health scientists, alternative healers, and is the author of a bestselling memoir, *Brave New Medicine: A Doctor's Unconventional Path to Healing Her Autoimmune Illness*.

Since 2014, she has been a student of Zhineng Qigong, and has organized and taught workshops for up to 1,000 people. In 2022, she received her teacher certification in Mingjue practice under Teacher Wei, and served as an organizer and writer for The World Consciousness Community.

CONTENTS

EDITOR'S PREFACE

"How can I have more freedom in my life?"

"How can I have more freedom in my body?"

These questions lie at the heart of the human experience. They also lie at the heart of Mingjue Gongfu, or Pure Consciousness training.

Over the past twenty years, I have been treating patients who have wrestled with these questions, not as mental concepts but deep within their cells. Spanning underserved and privileged communities alike, they have endured unspeakable traumas and harrowing health conditions. As an American-trained doctor of internal medicine – a specialist in chronic diseases – I have witnessed their suffering with a fierce desire to heal their illnesses.

Up until I embarked on Mingjue Gongfu practices, however, I hadn't realized the extent, hidden below this fierce and well-meaning desire, of the reservoir of grief, resistance, and fear. My entire life's path was fueled by a determination to *not* accept suffering, to fight it with everything I had. In a contracted state, I was not only limiting my capacity to be a healing presence for others, but for myself, too.

My Personal Journey

The resistance I had toward generalized suffering was entangled with my own. In 2005, as a young doctor and a new mother, I was stricken with complex chronic conditions that affected my immune, hormone, digestive, and nervous systems, leaving me debilitated for the greater part of a decade. This stressed my marriage to the breaking point. And the paradigm in which I had trained offered little to no solutions.

To say that I was drawn to Zhineng Qigong would not be true. Desperation opens minds like nothing else, and this was one of Desperation's greatest gifts to me. My adventure began in 2014, meaning it took me nine challenging years to find Zhineng Qigong. Or perhaps, it found me. That is, Mingjue, or Pure Consciousness, was slowly making its way back to itself.

Now, another nine years later, I reflect back: I started with fifteen minutes a day of what I considered an obligatory, medical "mind-body rehabilitation exercise." But I was diligent, and the teachings felt, at once, novel and ancient. At some point, qigong came to feel like eating; if I went too long without it, I hungered for it. And here was the wild part: the healing happened as a side-effect, without trying. By Western science standards, my healing was classified as a "radical remission," an outcome that defied statistical odds. For Zhineng Qigong, it was nothing special — simply opening to and coming into resonance with the healing laws of nature.

What is Zhineng Qigong?

Qigong is an embodied consciousness practice that aims to transform consciousness, qi (energy), and the body, both to heal and grow in wisdom. Originating from indigenous traditions in ancient China, qigong has continued to evolve as humanity and cultures have evolved. A substantial body of scientific evidence now validates its healing effects on the immune system, inflammation, bone density, cardiovascular disease, physical function, emotional wellbeing, among other significant improvements in quality of life.

There are hundreds of lineages of qigong. In the early 1980s, Dr. Pang Ming founded the lineage of Zhineng Qigong (zhì 智 means "wisdom", néng 能 means "abilities"). Dr. Pang had trained under several grandmasters, studied both Eastern and Western medicine, and mastered several forms of martial arts. In this new lineage, he drew from the teachings and practices of many traditions — including Daoism (Taoism), Buddhism, Confucianism, medical qigong, martial arts, folk qigong, contemporary science, medicine, and philosophy.

Zhineng Qigong theories and practices aim to describe the laws of the universe and humanity, as well as to consolidate them into a single system for vitality, health, and inner peace. Recognizing the role of modern science to enhance the validity and accessibility of qigong, Dr. Pang founded the Huaxia Zhineng Qigong Center ("Medicineless Hospital") in China, observing and recording the healing outcomes of the students. "Miracle" after miracle occurred, in many whose conditions were deemed incurable or terminal by their doctors.

Why Mingjue Gongfu?

The core teaching of Zhineng Qigong is conscious transformation. But after decades of teaching tens of thousands of students, Dr. Pang observed many becoming stuck. Their diligence to practice had turned into attachments — whether it be to the theories, methods, or powerful sensations of qi (energy) — and their personal lives and relationships were not necessarily harmonizing either.

So Dr. Pang began to emphasize Mingjue Gongfu, or Pure Consciousness training. Mastering the body and mastering energy, he taught, come by mastering the mind. When we practice for and from something much bigger than ourselves — the collective field — we come closer to our essence, enlarge our hearts, and reduce the risks of the small self thinking it is the master. We can also release our attachments to practice in a freer state. So, practicing Zhineng Qigong from a Mingjue state can benefit not just the practitioner; it amplifies the wellbeing of others, humanity at large, and the natural world.

How This Book is Organized

When I began Teacher Wei's Mingjue courses in 2021, it was his second year to offer his Mingjue Gongfu courses through The World Consciousness Community. The contents of this book are adapted from the direct transcriptions of the first two years. At the time, generous organizers and translators from around the world were transcribing his teachings into multiple languages. The material could be dense, however, and there was no go-to reference book for Mingjue Theory or Mingjue meditation practices.

This book is intended as a companion text to Teacher Wei's courses. There is a lot of material, some of which can feel complex. The simplicity, though, is the common thread woven through all the theories and methods: Mingjue. As you will learn, Mingjue is the autonomous observer within you and every other individual. Awakening this inner observer is inextricably linked to the healing of your thoughts, emotions, and body.

Mingjue is also the collective consciousness. This means that, when we practice Mingjue as a community, informed by universal love and infused with universal peace, we are co-creating and co-cultivating a powerful, unified qi and information field. Each individual consciousness is improved by connecting with the collective field. Likewise, the collective field is enhanced by every individual's awakening state.

There are two main sections: Part 1 covers the theories and Part 2, the methods and practices. The two sections complement and potentiate each other. They may also be used to complement Dr. Pang's foundational books, *Hunyuan Entirety Theory* and *The Methods of Zhineng Qigong Science* (available as ebooks for purchase at www.daohearts.com/books).

For concepts that might feel abstract or unclear, you can nonetheless receive them as a transmission, trusting that your energy and information are already changing. Like other books of enduring wisdom, this book may be read again and again; each time, you will likely discover new truths and understanding.

A few remarks on the text: when the word "qigong" appears in this book, it refers to the specific lineage of Zhineng Qigong. Foreign words are largely italicized only upon first introduction. In Chinese, the script is based on pictograms and ideograms; there is no such option as capitalization or not. In this book, the theories, concepts, and practice methods specific to Zhineng Qigong and Mingjue Gongfu are capitalized. Energy points, palaces, and gates are also capitalized for ease of recognition.

Deepest gratitude to ĀnYuè (A. Barrios Camponovo) of Uruguay-Spain and Susan Drouilhet of the U.S. for their brilliant minds, devoted hearts, and skilled hands on the final editing and formatting of this book.

An Experiment in Quantum Awakening and Healing

As I was about to embark on this path, I knew these were the precise lessons I had yet to learn in my own life and work. I did not know, though, that Mingjue Gongfu intersected with the leading edge of neuroscience and quantum physics.

Research studies from organizations like HeartMath Institute in the U.S. have been measuring the power of consciousness and energy fields. They found, for example, when someone feels anxious, scared, or frustrated, the heart rhythms become chaotic and irregular, as do the brain waves. Conversely, a state of calm, gratitude, or compassion brings the heart and brain rhythms into regular, smooth patterns — a state of energetic flow called "coherence," which is distinct from simple relaxation. When we are in coherence, our bodies function optimally and healing happens naturally.

What's more, HeartMath scientists measured the electromagnetic field of the human heart to extend some six to eight feet outward. While in a state of coherence, someone can bring others in his or her field into coherence, thereby amplifying the healing potential of everyone in the field.

Imagine ten people in coherence in a single space. Or fifty. And what if the subtler, as-of-yet immeasurable energies worked similarly? For millennia, qigong practitioners have known the power of this conscious, universe-sized field by direct experience. So imagine a hundred people in coherence across vast distances. A thousand. A million. As I have now tasted firsthand, qigong as a collective field isn't a private mind-body exercise. It is a bold experiment in quantum healing, harmony, and love.

In this spirit, Teacher Wei founded The World Consciousness Community and began amplifying his Mingjue Gongfu courses. The Mingjue state is the foundation for all the dynamic movement forms. He always reminds us: *Who* is choosing to practice? *Who* is initiating the movements? *Who* is inhabiting the body, even as it remains independent, enabling us to be *in* our bodies and the world, but not *of* them? *Who* is connected to all other consciousnesses through the collective field?

And for me, in my healing work, *Who* is witnessing the suffering, with an open heart? *Who* is making clinical recommendations even as she surrenders to a greater, collective intelligence?

Pure Consciousness — the true *I*. The true *we*.

When we return home to our true selves, the "inner work" of Mingjue and qigong becomes "inner play." We practice in a free state. We live our lives in a free state. We love ourselves, others, and the world in a free state.

"Always look *at* your observer," says Teacher Wei, "and always look *from* your observer. Then you will experience freedom."

We invite you to join us in this quantum experiment. And we hope this book can support you in your health and wellbeing.

Cynthia Li, MD
Berkeley, CA, USA

Xin Xiang Shi Cheng

In this universal collective field,
what is born from your pure heart is successfully realized.

PART 1:
THEORY

THE FOUNDATION:
PRACTICING IN COMMUNITY

In the courses of The World Consciousness Community, the community practices as one. The World Consciousness Community practices as a collective field, rooted in love. When students and teachers practice together **in this universal collective field, everyone is equal** — because in the field, everyone has the same potential and everyone supports each other.

From Dr. Pang:

Only those who work for the wellbeing and evolution of humankind can make their personal life complete and happy.

If you want to be happy, you must work for the happiness of all people. If you only practice for yourself, the beautiful feeling will not be enough. But when you rise to a higher level, connect consciously with the world, and your attitude becomes "I practice for the world," your heart expands and your happiness rises to another level.

Individual and collective practice benefits the world. As each of us comes together to practice, the world consciousness field grows stronger and stronger. Its resonance increasingly influences others, and others can connect with our collective Mingjue field. Some may come to practice with us without knowing why. Everyone and anyone can benefit from the healing effects of the consciousness field because we are one entirety.

> When we practice,
> we don't just practice for ourselves.
> We practice as
> the whole collective consciousness field
> — all hearts merged as one.

Why Practice in The World Consciousness Community?

1. To learn high-level laws of life and of the universe.

2. To receive support from community members doing the same.

3. The community consciousness field can help your consciousness become more stable, pure, and positive.

4. The community consciousness field can support the qi field in and around your cells, organs, and body, and also around your family, to become more harmonious and strong.

5. The community consciousness field can give you power. Your social relationships can become more harmonious, your life can become safer and more successful, and you can more readily attain health, peace, happiness, and freedom.

6. The community consciousness field can support you to practice more deeply and to more readily improve your quality of life.

7. When you merge yourself into the community consciousness field, your worldview can change, your heart can open more, your True Self and universal love can gradually appear. In turn, your transformations can intensify the world consciousness field, thus realizing your life together with all the community members in the infinite entirety (oneness).

8. Group practice in the community can help you develop self-discipline.

PRINCIPLES IN THE WORLD CONSCIOUSNESS COMMUNITY

1. Everyone is welcome.

2. Relationships between members are as brother, sister, teacher, and student.

3. Each member recognizes their individual role in connecting to and cultivating the collective field for the benefit of their own consciousness, the qi field, as well as their family's qi field.

4. All members commit to uniting, supporting each other, and sending love to enhance the world consciousness field and build a harmonious life as their life's mission. During practice, all members consciously connect to each other with Mingjue universal love.

5. Organizers and teachers support the members to merge with the collective consciousness field for the benefit of their lives, which in turn enhances the collective field.

6. Organizers and teachers commit to work together to build a strong, global field of consciousness, information, and qi.

7. Everyone commits to loving self, family, world, and all of humanity.

8. Everyone commits to maintain harmony with and between each other.

> Practice is the way to a free state of life.
> We cultivate a good attitude and entirety state.
> At the same time, in society,
> we respect the rules of a dualistic world.

A NOTE ON TRUST

"How can I come to trust something that I don't?"

Many people come to Zhineng Qigong and Mingjue Gongfu with questions on trust. Sometimes it is skepticism about the theories and methods, or doubting the healing potential of the consciousness-qi field. Other times, it is a lack of trust toward themselves — that they cannot practice well, that everyone except them can experience deep healing and awakening, or that they are not worthy of such transformation and unconditional love. Teacher Wei often hears from students, "I want to trust myself, but I cannot."

This inability to trust the methods and ourselves comes from the ego mind (or the reference framework), where trust is always conditional and relative. It's a circumstantial kind of trust like, "If I have enough of this [fill in the blank: security, health, beauty, money, food, prestige, a powerful life partner, a good family, a great job…], then I will trust life." But what lies on the other side of conditional trust? Fear. Anxiety. Doubt. So conditional trust, well, cannot be trusted. It not only limits our potential to heal, but also our capacity to trust others and trust ourselves.

Zhineng Qigong and Mingjue Gongfu can support us to develop more trust, for example, by explaining the scientific theories and health benefits of many practitioners — as are contained in this book. This can be useful for new and seasoned students alike.

Truly lasting trust, however, must come from within — from everyone's own direct experiences.

Teacher Wei illustrates this with a vignette:

Two people contract the Covid-19 virus. One person feels the discomfort, endures the symptoms, rests, maybe takes some medicines, and waits for recovery. Another person feels similar symptoms, but he also observes them and keeps his consciousness free, sending "good" (coherent, harmonious) information to the body: "This is very difficult, but I am not my symptoms. I will practice qigong to make my blood and qi flow well!"

The first person is living life in a passive state. Life is already full of enough challenges! So why create more challenges by succumbing to disharmonious information? The second person is living from an active state. And because qi (energy) and matter (the body) follow the information of consciousness, these two states are very different. Their consequences are very different, too.

When you experience benefits like this from an active state, your trust can grow. You must choose to practice, though. No one else can make that decision for you. **The deepest level of trust emerges more subtly**: through conscious practice, you come to realize that you — or Mingjue (Pure Consciousness) — are the master, creator, and observer of your life. This means that gradually, or sometimes quite radically, you have gone beyond the ego mind (or reference framework) and its conditional states. Universal energy will follow your consciousness to support your life.

This doesn't guarantee that life will be easy and comfortable. It means that, no matter what life presents, you can respond with compassion and clarity; you will not lose yourself to external triggers, bodily sensations, or other people; and you know who you are — unshakable Mingjue love.

If, after practicing for a while, you still find yourself lacking trust, open your heart to other Mingjue Gongfu students. Listen to what their experiences have been and how they came to trust the practices and themselves more. Also, take some time to pause, ask yourself, and truly experience inside your body the answer to this essential question:

Who is the "I" who is wanting or seeking more trust?

QI AND QIGONG

In order to understand Mingjue, it is important to first have a basic understanding of *qi* and energy.

WHAT IS QI 氣?

Qi (pronounced "chee") is the Chinese word for life force energy. Generally speaking, qi is the basic substance of the universe. Everything is made *of* qi. Everything is made *by* qi. Often, qi is used to simply mean "energy."

Qi can be invisible — "the formless realm" — or visible — "form" or "matter." Invisible qi fills the empty space of the universe and also permeates all matter. There are different levels and kinds of invisible qi. Electricity, magnetism, radiation, and quantum energy are a few examples.

Everything in the universe is the vibration of energy. Qi converts into matter and matter converts into energy.

"Qi" is often used in the following two phrases:

1. **The Qi Body** — the physical body is a concentrated or condensed qi space. When qi is very concentrated, we call it a physical body with a form, but it is still qi. Because of its density, qi bodies are relatively stable.

   Consciousness is a special kind of qi space. It is very pure and very fine.

   In Mingjue Gongfu, when your consciousness observes and merges with the inner space of your qi body, part by part, your consciousness can learn to go beyond the physical dimension of your body. You can even come to feel and see the qi moving and flowing inside your body.

2. **The Qi Field** — there is an energetic field inside and around the qi body. In Zhineng Qigong, this is called the "qi field." With practice, this qi field can become finer and finer.

   Overall, this field is relatively stable. It stays with you.

Your consciousness can help to maintain and enhance this qi field by gathering invisible qi from the universe into the body. As it condenses, this invisible qi becomes manifest in physical form.

Training your consciousness to stay centered and connected to your body's core can strengthen the qi field inside and around your body.

WHAT IS QIGONG 氣功?

Gong means work. So qigong is the work or effort to cultivate qi, or life force energy.

Qigong Includes Four Elements:

1. **Theory** — this includes the laws of the universe and the laws of life. Students learn how to use qi to transform their lives. Qigong theory is used to teach and guide; it is never used to control, argue, or fight.

2. **Methods** — from the theories, a series of movements and meditations are developed to practice qi, strengthen the body, and train the mind.

3. **Practice** — without practice, there is no qigong. Students must learn to directly experience the laws of the universe and life. This requires a deep commitment from the heart, a practice plan, and self-discipline.

4. **Application** — the wisdom and abilities that result from a regular qigong practice can transform lives, relationships, and the world. Translating the theories and methods into daily life is the real practice.

THEORIES AND METHODS GO HAND IN HAND

Studying Theories Transforms Your Consciousness

The theories provide a framework for understanding human nature (including health and healing), life, and the universe. As you study, you can gain more awareness and agency over the choices you make in your daily life.

The theories can change old, conditioned thinking patterns and thereby change, little by little, your inner programming. This change in consciousness changes the energy (qi) of your body, which can change the state of your health, relationships, and whole life.

Dr. Pang often said that teaching and learning are also "practices" — a high-level practice. That is, the information contained in the theories is a kind of transformation. Sometimes, when certain pieces of information ring true for someone, an epiphany or sudden change can happen.

Practicing the Methods Enhances Healing and Awakening

To complement the theories, Zhineng Qigong also teaches static meditations (standing or sitting) and dynamic methods (movement techniques) to transform the mind and body. By practicing these embodied meditations, you can activate your potential to heal acute and chronic health challenges that affect you physically, mentally, or emotionally. You can also learn to heal others.

The methods also teach the development of consciousness, including extrasensory perceptions, intuition, and paranormal abilities — what Zhineng Qigong calls "super abilities."

Mingjue Qigong Theory Aims to:

- Teach students (and never to control them)
- Cultivate a peaceful state of oneness
- Transform qi
- Support consciousness in coming to the True Self (Yiyuanti)

When your consciousness can master the body, you can master your life, your health, and your world.

HUN YUAN QI 混元氣

Hun Yuan Qi is the energy of everything in the universe.

The different levels of Hun Yuan Qi:

- Original Hun Yuan Qi — ubiquitous qi that is very pure, fine, and subtle.
- Hun Yuan Qi of everything — this qi includes all physical matter and formless energy.
- Human Hun Yuan Qi — the entire state of the body's energy and consciousness.
- Consciousness Hun Yuan Qi or Yiyuanti — the pure qi field of the brain and nerve cells.

Hun Yuan Qi is in our bodies, in the mountains, the earth, the moon, the sun, and in the whole of empty space.

Hun means to merge. *Yuan* means oneness. *Hun Yuan* means to merge and become one. *Hun Yuan* emphasizes that different energy is always merging, transforming, and becoming one.

Hun Yuan Qi can also be simply referred to as qi.

In the general sense, qi refers to formless substances.

In the more precise sense, qi is all the form and formless substances, because the qi of form (matter) is gathered from the formless qi.

The Formless Qi Realm

Modern science estimates that 95-96% of the universe is comprised of invisible substances—dark matter and dark energy. In any given second, there are thousands of particles of dark matter moving throughout the human body.

In qigong, this is called "universal qi," and it is in continuous flow and movement. Universal qi is described as *kong kong dang dang, huang huang hu hu*, which means **"empty but not empty."** It may seem empty, but is actually very subtle, very fine qi.

The nervous system of the human body is not wired to perceive or sense this subtle energy. But our consciousness can learn to observe and experience universal qi. It is qualitatively different from sensing qi with the body's five senses — which is a rougher, denser feeling of qi.

Physical Material Qi

All the (visible, physical) forms in the universe are also qi — *concentrated* or *condensed* qi. When formless qi becomes very concentrated, it becomes "form."

The universe contains information — like an infinite database — and the information has a kind of order to it — like a program. Every "thing" is based on the information/program that it contains. For example, human beings are formed by the combination of the information of their genetic code, the information contained in their consciousness, and also by qi. Similarly, in the vast universe, there is a high-level, pure qi merging together with its information.

In short, information gathers formless qi, condenses, and organizes into form.

It is important to know that the form and formless qi are always merging and transforming (*hunhua*) into each other. **Merging and transforming occur at the same time.**

> Form and formless
> are always
> merging and transforming.

HUN YUAN LING TONG

"Hun Yuan Ling Tong" is a foundational mantra of Zhineng Qigong that draws upon the power of Hun Yuan Qi.

Hun Yuan means that everything merges and harmonizes together, becoming one.

Ling means the pure, clear consciousness state that can readily receive and send (transmit) information effectively.

Tong means to become completely harmonious and open — a free-flowing state in which there are no blockages.

Together, *Ling Tong* means the awakening consciousness feels everything becoming beautiful and good.

When you say or hear *Hun Yuan Ling Tong,* your consciousness can directly receive this high-level information: "Everything is good and in harmony." Your consciousness increases in power, you trust your consciousness more, and everything is good — family, society, the natural world, and the entirety of it all.

Hun Yuan Ling Tong

Can you feel how changes are already happening?

Wei Qifeng's calligraphy

HUMAN HUN YUAN QI

Human Hun Yuan Qi is contained in and transmitted through various energy centers, points, and meridian channels. There are three energy centers and three important palaces.

Three Energy Centers: the Dantians

In Qigong Theory, a Dantian is a space in the body that has a high concentration of qi — it is therefore called an energy center. The human body has three, each with a different location and functions.

Although each Dantian is depicted as its own energy center, the three Dantians and their qi all merge together and spread throughout the body.

1. Lower Dantian — the energy space in the abdomen

2. Middle Dantian — the energy space in the chest

3. Upper Dantian — the energy space in the head*

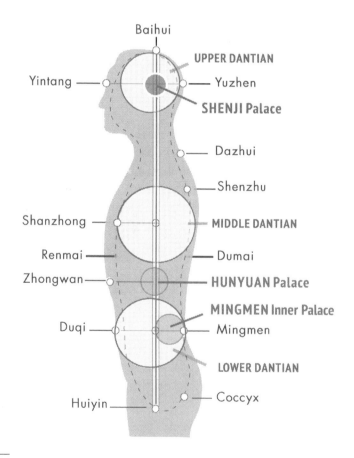

---

* See more details in Part 2: Methods and Practices

QI FIELD: CHARACTERISTICS AND FUNCTIONS

All material things, including the human body, have invisible qi within and around them — this is the qi field. Smaller things, like internal organs and cells, have their own qi fields within and around them. Larger things, like planets also have their own qi fields.

When people gather together, they combine their individual qi fields to form a big collective field.

Everything in the universe, from micro to macro, can come together, merging and forming the qi field of the whole universe.

The qi field is both a concept and a reality.

RELATIONSHIP BETWEEN THE QI FIELD AND MATTER

The Qi Field and Matter Are Connected

The qi field of a human being can form a single, larger qi field with others. If the qi of one person's body becomes stronger, his qi field becomes stronger. Conversely, when the qi field becomes stronger, the body also becomes stronger.

A tumor in the body also has a qi field. When Zhineng Qigong practitioners apply healing to a tumor, what happens is that the tumor's qi field disperses and the tumor consequently diminishes in size. This happens due to a transformation of qi between the form and formless. In other words, the physical form changes into invisible qi — it becomes part of the qi field.

A helpful metaphor: when ice changes into steam, it will quickly disappear. Even during very cold winters, if you hold a piece of ice in the wind, the ice will become smaller and smaller and eventually disappear.

Energy Transforms Into Matter (and Vice Versa)

Sometimes this conversion can happen very quickly. For example, when consciousness sends information to a tumor, the tumor can transform into invisible qi and disappear.

In the example of the tumor (or any other form of matter), it is important to realize that there is the physical form and the qi field of that particular thing. For tumors, even if the physical tumor disappears, its qi field can remain; in other words, the tumor's energy has not completely dispersed. In these cases, after certain information has been gathered by the residual qi field over a period of time, the tumor can return.

So it is important to continuously practice, to stay open in that space, and to send good information to that space. For example, doing Open and Close* to transform it many times, until the information in that space has become completely healthy.

Qi Field Changes Affect the Physical Form (and Vice Versa)

When the qi field changes, the form changes in response. When the form changes, the qi field also changes.

Does the Qi Field of Others Influence Me?

This is a common question, especially from highly sensitive people: "When we merge with each other, I am afraid the other person's negative qi can influence me."

There is nothing to fear. The qi field of each person is connected to his or her self-form (the body). Generally, everybody's qi field follows him- or herself. If it happens that someone's qi field merges with that of another person — for example, if someone else's qi field is very large (one or two meters wide) and you sit close to and even inside her qi field, the information in your qi field will transform a little, from her large qi field. Your qi field, however, still retains strong self-information. So when you separate, each person's qi field follows the self. While people can influence each other's qi fields, it is not long-lasting. It is not necessary to protect against this.

As Mingjue students, you practice to strengthen and stabilize your qi field. It is important to build confidence and trust in yourself.

If you sense someone else's pain, this is not due to that person's qi field. It is due to your consciousness receiving the information of that person's problems; through bodily sensations, your consciousness is showing you the problem areas of that person. You may then doubt or worry that the pain or problem has entered your body. This is not true.

However, if you continue to fear or worry about that sensation or signal of pain, your consciousness can continuously re-create the painful sensations in your body. This is when it can become a problem, because your consciousness now has made that your own information. This is a testament to how powerful your consciousness is.

A New Framework

If you experience challenges, problems, or negative information from someone else, you can think this instead: "My consciousness just received some information from someone else. This is not my problem and that problem cannot enter my body. Everything is fine." Later, you can change your conditioned reaction: you can know someone else's problem, but there will be no need for the symptom to show itself in your body. You no longer need to create the sensations.

* See Part 2: Methods and Practices

THE INFORMATION FIELD

In reality, the qi field, consciousness field, and information field are all one.

In the world of nature, for example, the qi in and around a tree is one qi field. The tree has its natural information field — that is, the internal information that codes for the tree and its life (there is no consciousness field with trees).

For humanity, these three fields form an entirety — and the consciousness field is the essence. The consciousness field changes the qi field. While the consciousness field of each individual is finite, a stronger, larger consciousness field results with the consciousnesses of many people coming together. When they send the same information, this forms a strong information field.

For example, when everyone thinks, "Haola!" an information field is formed. **The information field is actually within the consciousness field**, because consciousness is what is sending this information.

QI-LEVEL EMPTINESS, PEACE, HARMONY

Many of us place our attention and energy on the physical level of life and become fixated by them: our physical bodies, possessions, money, jobs, or other people. These attachments can create internal qi blockages. Suffering can ensue. Unconditional love becomes impossible.

Fear is created by our attachments on the material world and the physical body. Our five senses generate sensations in the body, creating a reference framework through which we interpret life events.

However, the practice of observing at an increasingly deeper level can bring inner peace and openness. This is a direct result of merging with the universe. You become the universe; you become an infinite emptiness. The more you focus on the infinite universal qi and experience it, the less you focus and fixate on the physical world and the physical body. Your focus naturally changes.

Since **universal qi is an infinite entirety** (or state of oneness), this state is very pure, very even. The mind does not get attached to any specific thing(s) and the heart feels open. There is no resistance. It is a reality in which everything can change. In other words, **there is nothing that can _not_ change.** It is thereby a state released of any and all attachments. Without attachments, fear naturally diminishes. Ultimately, the fear diminishes to a point of fearlessness. From this harmonious entirety state, unconditional love and true liberation arise.

Q: Who is the master of this Qi Entirety state?

A: Mingjue. Our Pure Consciousness.

MINGJUE AWAKENING

WHAT IS MINGJUE 明觉?

Ming means clear or pure. *Jue* means observer or observation. In simplest terms, Mingjue means a state of self-aware consciousness.

The term "Mingjue" is an expansive state of awareness that includes both individual consciousness and the collective consciousness field. There are many different ways to describe Mingjue:

- **The self-aware inner observer** (or simply "the observer" or "the inner observer") — within each individual, there is an internal observer.

- **The Self who knows Itself** — there is also a universal consciousness that can reflect itself. The inner observer within each individual can merge with this universal consciousness (also called "the collective consciousness field") and therefore contribute to making the universe conscious. This is also Mingjue.

- **Awakened Pure Consciousness** — the consciousness who is aware of itself.

In Mingjue Gongfu, Mingjue is the master of all the practice methods.

Mingjue as a State of Being

There is Mingjue the observer, then there is the Mingjue state. When the inner observer comes to observe itself, we call this the Mingjue state. It is naturally peaceful, as if consciousness has returned home to itself.

> Individual Mingjue consciousnesses
> make up the collective field.
> The collective consciousness field
> is also in everyone's Mingjue.

This Pure Consciousness state goes beyond all sensations, thoughts, ideas, and emotions, and can be characterized as:

- Pure, harmonious, and clear

- Oneness, or an entirety state (no separation or duality)

- Universal love, peace, and happiness

Mingjue as a Process

"Mingjue" can also be used to describe the progressive development of the inner observer at different stages. For example, when the observer is just beginning to observe itself, we call it Mingjue. At the highest level, we also call it Mingjue. This reflects different levels of awareness. It is all Mingjue.

In our daily lives, most of us are not aware of the presence of the inner observer. But in actuality, the observer is always present. When the observer always knows itself and always is itself — this awakened state is the essence of the following Chinese saying:

明觉常在

Ming Jue Chang Zai: Keep your Mingjue state always in the present moment.

To awaken the inner observer, regular practice is necessary. When the observer comes to observe itself, you know you are the pure observer and nothing can distract or trigger you from this awareness.

Yiyuanti — True Self or enlightenment — can be thought of as the highest level of Mingjue state. With steady practice, Mingjue grows in stability, independence, and purity, ultimately leading to enlightenment and inner freedom.

Ming Jue Chang Zai

Mingjue Gongfu

Gongfu (sometimes spelled "kung fu") means both the duration and the abilities of training.

- Gongfu is the ability to create a harmonious entirety state.
- Gongfu is a function of Mingjue consciousness.

In Mingjue Gongfu, the training is to become a master of your life and health. **Mingjue Gongfu is a way of loving yourself**. And loving yourself benefits not just your life, but the love you exude then benefits your family and community, all human beings, and the natural world.

Gongfu manifests in the body as an increase in qi, or life force energy. In other words, gongfu can increase your strength, flexibility, power, and vitality (think: Bruce Lee and other kung fu masters).

Gongfu can also manifest in your work and in your specific skills or talents. After a long time of training, you can become highly skilled in those areas.

Gongfu is applied to the practice of dynamic methods (movements and practice forms), meditations, and the work and tasks of daily life. Cleaning the yard, for example, is a gongfu practice for monks. As students of Zhineng Qigong, you are also called to practice in and throughout your daily life.

All gongfu, however, comes from your consciousness. The level of consciousness is different for different people and can vary from time to time. So we call this Mingjue Gongfu.

Mingjue Gongfu can support your consciousness to:

- Become more stable, pure, and wise
- Increase its potential
- Develop certain "super abilities" like intuition and extrasensory perceptions

Mingjue meditation and deep internal observation provide a path for consciousness to integrate with the body. Integrating mind and body for a few minutes is easy; this is not real gongfu. Gongfu means training the mind to stay in that state for a long time.

Can consciousness remain merged with the qi body during daily tasks, like while doing household chores? Can consciousness stay connected to the breath and continue observing itself while driving or talking with others? If so, this is a high level of gongfu.

Everything you do in the world requires some effort. Changing your life requires effort. However, it's important to relax as much as possible and enjoy the Mingjue Gongfu practice itself.

How is Mingjue Gongfu a Qigong Practice?

Mingjue Gongfu practice is different from general qigong practice because the primary focus is not the methods, but on consciousness — training the mind. Mingjue Gongfu practitioners understand that diligent training and good discipline are necessary; and that all dynamic methods are just tools, meant to be used in a free consciousness state.

You may wonder what Mingjue has to do with qigong: "Don't we need to practice cultivating qi (energy)?"

Teacher Wei: "If we don't cultivate Mingjue consciousness, our egos can use qi to become more powerful and more misguided. If our qi increases from qigong practice but we are practicing from an ego state, it can create disharmony. This is not qigong at its essence."

Important: Qi is neutral, in your body and in the universe. How you use qi matters more. And what matters the most is what you connect to when you practice, during the practice itself and throughout your days.

Two Levels of Mingjue Gongfu

1. When Mingjue can remain stable — continuously developing and maintaining Mingjue for a long time, and even remaining this way in daily activities. The observer becomes increasingly clearer.

2. When Mingjue applies its functions to other things — for example, Mingjue works on practicing qigong methods, using its functions to improve the body, qi, or someone else's health or consciousness state. Mingjue can also apply its function on relationships and society. Even as Mingjue observes externally, Mingjue never loses itself to other events or people.

How Mingjue Gongfu Differs From Other Awareness Practices

- Hun Yuan Entirety Theory is the foundation.
- The systematic methods integrate the body, qi, and consciousness into one practice.

- Mingjue Gongfu can enhance both extrasensory perceptions and the wisdom of consciousness.

- The Mingjue state can transform and purify the body, the mind, and the world.

- Mingjue practice is informed by scientific theory — which sets it apart from traditional religious ideas.

- Mingjue practice cultivates a strong worldwide, high-level consciousness field to support individual Mingjue states.

Healing a Divided Consciousness

Modern society provides a lot of information that divides human consciousness. Daily life is often hectic and stressful. People form many external attachments and lose themselves to these attachments. This divided consciousness can result in a lot of tension, energy depletion, and fatigue. People become less able to manage their lives and to live optimally.

Through Mingjue practice, anyone can learn to go beyond old, conditioned thinking patterns — beyond conflict and fear.

Establishing a Good Foundation

Since Mingjue is the master of this practice, Mingjue has to be in the best state.

Many Zhineng Qigong students have spent many years practicing different dynamic methods – like Level 1 (Lift Qi Up, Pour Qi Down) or Level 2 (Body Mind) – and keep their focus on the techniques or process of the methods. They do not develop the gongfu of observing deeper and deeper within. So even after many years and increased physical skill, the depth of their observation and their states of consciousness remain the relatively unchanged.

How to move beyond this? Here are two simple steps:

1. Keep a simple focus. Release any questions — it is important, especially at the beginning of your training, to refrain from asking questions. This means not just withholding them, but releasing them. Can you surrender the need to know? This helps to cultivate a simple focus and a good, clear mind state. Too many questions can divide the consciousness state and serve as a distraction.

2. Observe. Then observe some more — to build a good foundation, it is important to prioritize observation. Initially, when people start to practice Mingjue Gongfu, they may notice their inner observer becoming stronger. Over time, as a natural shift of continually observing the body at increasingly subtler and deeper levels, this inner observer can come to observe itself.

Some of you may think: "I always merge my consciousness with the qi body. It doesn't feel like anything." It is important to realize this is the ego mind thinking. When you can observe that it is the ego mind thinking that, this observation is from Mingjue.

This training alone — of deep observation — can be practiced for many years.

> How deep can your consciousness
> merge with your body?

The Traditional Way of Building a Good Foundation

In the past, when masters worked more directly with their students in smaller groups, this level of Mingjue wasn't taught until a good foundation was established by the students — which usually took many years. A "good foundation" has to do with their states of consciousness. Teachers and masters would not teach the high-level secrets in the beginning.

They would first wait for their students to open their hearts. To have an open heart meant serving others for the benefit of society. An open heart is a good and respectful heart.

The masters would find different ways to train their students to loosen the grip of their ego minds. Train, train, train, over and over again, greater and greater surrender of the ego, letting go of attachments to many different things. At some point, the students would come to experience almost no emotions. It might appear that they had given up everything from the material world and only wanted to discover who they were. That nothing else was important — fame, the game of life, affections. A strong willpower would take hold and lead them toward enlightenment, their consciousnesses naturally becoming more peaceful. Then and only then would the master find his students' quality of heart ready and guide them to realize the True Self.

The Modern Way of Building a Good Foundation

Life's challenges serve to further train Mingjue abilities. When trials come, someone who has a good understanding and deep trust of Mingjue practice can experience life's trials as powerful trainings.

Perhaps after months of enjoying a relaxed Mingjue state and a beautiful life, difficult experiences emerge. Maybe a beloved friend or family member dies. Or a cherished belonging breaks. Or some health challenges or pain arises. Suddenly, the beautiful life is gone; or perhaps it is the Mingjue practice that has heightened the awareness of problems that weren't noticeable before.

Living and embracing life with all of its challenges are part of this training. If life was always easy and peaceful, students could not see their levels of stability and harmony. Their Mingjue Gongfu could not be tested. They could not see where their attachments are and where they have released former attachments.

When trials happen, some students give up hope, give up their practice, or forget the True Self. Everyone has a choice in how to respond. You have a choice in how to respond. And you can choose to trust your Mingjue, to focus on Mingjue, and to keep Mingjue stable.

Important: Remember that you have the world consciousness field to support you. You are learning and growing together with all the other students and teachers in the field. This kind of collective mindset and experience can catalyze learning and growing.

> In today's world,
> life is the training ground.

Once Awakened, Mingjue is Hard to Lose

Once the observer awakens, it starts to grow. It grows through training and begins to recognize its own potential. When Mingjue love — the pure baby heart — appears, you can love unconditionally. When you love others from this pure baby heart, you also receive love from yourself and from the world at large.

Once you have experienced the Mingjue state, it becomes difficult to try to lose it. If you try to lose it, the more you will stay in Mingjue state.

Teacher Wei: "Take it step by step, don't hurry. You cannot grow up by just eating one meal. You need to eat a little every day."

Two Ways to Strengthen Willpower

1. By increasing the information inside your consciousness — this is the information level. Information needs to be regularly reviewed. Life's challenges can greatly strengthen the information because the information is directly applied and put into action.

2. By increasing your energy/qi — this is the energy level. Increasing the qi of the kidney system is especially important.

Overview of Mingjue Gongfu

1. Mingjue (or True Self, or Yiyuanti) is the essence of all human beings.

2. Mingjue Entirety — Mingjue merges with the qi body and the universe's infinite qi field to form a conscious universal field. It is the awakened life state of oneness. (See the subsequent section on Entirety Theory for more details.)

3. Universal love is the basic function of Mingjue. Being universal love is what creates beauty in individual lives and in the world.

4. The reference framework is a tool for Mingjue. It helps people to manage their daily lives. The reference framework of Zhineng Qigong — both the theories and the methods — is to build a centered, integrated Mingjue Entirety state.

The Benefits of Mingjue Gongfu

While Mingjue Gongfu has many benefits, the fundamental purpose for any practice is to receive information — or to grow in wisdom.

When the information changes, consciousness also changes, followed by changes in energy. Just believing isn't enough. It is essential to directly experience these changes. Only then can true transformation happen.

Basic gongfu: practicing to observe qi on a very subtle level. Later, coming to observe Pure Consciousness itself, which is the finest level of qi.

Mingjue Gongfu can support practitioners to:

1. Improve their complete life.

"Complete life" means that Mingjue Gongfu doesn't just improve the body's health and vitality, or just increase its energy level. "Complete life" includes the following three levels for each person:

- Physical (body)
- Qi (energy)
- Consciousness (mind and heart)

A complete life also includes relationships and all lived experiences.

It is easy to become fixated on the physical body — the sensations, the appearance, the changes — and fixated on the goal of healing. A common thought process is: "I must practice this method or that method in order to heal this or that." But this increases the risk of becoming fixated on the methods.

The methods and theories are just tools for realizing a beautiful, harmonious life, in which healing is a natural side-effect. "Healing without healing." So it is important to shift the focus. In so doing, the practice becomes flexible.

2. Go beyond the limitations of old conditioned patterns.

For beginners of qigong — many come to this practice because something in their lives isn't working for them any more. Perhaps a crisis of health, a relationship, or global stresses. Perhaps there's no crisis — they seek change from old, conditioned patterns or seek more inner peace, harmony, and freedom.

For seasoned practitioners — many have practiced for years or decades, but their practice may be limited to feelings and bodily sensations. The greater the qi and power experience, the greater they feel. Perhaps they have become healthier and stronger. But when the mind becomes attached to these sensations and goals, the attachments can become obstructions to the higher levels of practice.

Grandmaster Pang's wisdom — at the Huaxia Center ("Medicineless Qigong Hospital") in China, Dr. Pang always emphasized the need to transcend the feelings of the body or the sensations of qi. Otherwise, the mind risks "dying on the body," "dying on qi," or "dying on the intention."

Some practitioners risk becoming attached to Qigong Theory and qigong methods, or "dying on knowledge" and using knowledge to feel superiority or create division. Qigong Theory is important to study. But it's a reference framework — and any reference framework is just a tool.

3. Resolve social conflicts.

Today, a lot of mental attention and energy focuses on the material world (the world of "form"): fame, power, wealth, and affection. People lose touch with themselves, and the mind cannot come back to itself.

This is the root of many social conflicts. When the consciousness is fixed on the external, material world, it creates an undercurrent of separateness, division, and fear. This fear erupts as conflicts between countries, religions, and cultures.

4. Awaken humanity to peace and freedom.

Beyond individual and social benefits, the greater purpose of Mingjue Gongfu is to enhance human evolution, to elevate humanity to a higher level of consciousness. The practice of Mingjue can lead to the awakening of consciousness — to inner peace, freedom, and universal love. A high level of consciousness transforms the physical body and also the material world to create great harmony.

At a certain level of consciousness, practitioners recognize that all humans are one.

Mingjue in Daily Life

Mingjue Gongfu can express in many different ways and levels:

- Consciousness merges with the qi body and becomes one, with increasing effectiveness and stability — this results in confidence, courage, and health.

- Consciousness merges with universal qi and becomes one, with increasing effectiveness and stability — this results in peace and harmony.

- A fully autonomous consciousness — this is a high-level gongfu when your consciousness can merge with everything and also remain independent, so nothing can shake you.

- Relationships — how harmonious is your consciousness state in your relationships? When you interact with others, can you remain in a state of pure, unconditional love?

- A harmonious world — this, too, is an ability of consciousness. You can have a harmonious life, a harmonious family, and also have the ability to co-create a harmonious world.

Mingjue Gongfu as Healing

Mingjue Gongfu is also a kind of healing — a high level healing. Even without an explicit intention, healing can happen as a natural side-effect. So it is often called "healing without healing."

When Mingjue merges with your qi body, your internal qi naturally becomes stronger. This is why, by remaining in a good Mingjue state, you are also taking care of your health and healing.

The "Self" State

In the early stages of Mingjue practice, students usually experience a duality, a split: "The observer observes itself." There is a subject and an object. This is due to the conditioned reference framework of duality. In reality, there is no division.

Over time, as you continue to observe the self, you come to a point when the intention of observing the self disappears. The subject and object of the observer disappear. You have arrived at the "self state": the observer is clearly in this universe and is one with the universe.

How this might manifest: At some point, when your inner space is ripe, an event or person might challenge or trigger you. Instead of trying to stay in Mingjue state, you simply are in Mingjue state. The duality disappears. The boundary of observation disappears. There is no observer anymore, and no observation either. You have become yourself. At this point, the Mingjue state remains without the need for the intention to maintain the state. It is just there.

When you observe and forget the intention, there is no effort anymore. There is no attachment to the external world. There is no attachment to the observer. You do not need to think, "I am Mingjue." You do not need to find Mingjue or attach to Mingjue.

You are the observer.

You are.

HOW TO HOLD INTENTION

For beginners — it is important to hold a slight intention for consistent training and commitment. At some point, when you have practiced enough, you can stay focused at a very pure level without an intention. But before you have arrived at this level, you should keep an intention in order to keep your consciousness focused, not scattered.

For both beginners and seasoned practitioners: It is important to **relax your intention.** When you practice either dynamic (moving) or static qigong methods, your intentions should be focused but light. Train to keep your mind empty, thinking of nothing else but the practice. This is very important!

If your intention is too strong, it becomes an attachment, which can bring bodily (Hun Yuan) qi into the level of consciousness — your brain can become heavy or tense.

For seasoned practitioners — even when you feel you have reached the level of complete emptiness — *kong kong dang dang huang huang hu hu* ("empty but not empty") — your consciousness still can be scattered. Train to observe at an ever deeper and deeper level.

Even if there is no intention at the level of complete emptiness, some random thoughts or imaginations may still emerge. This is a comfortable and free state because the random thoughts are not fixed or blocked; they are flowing. All kinds of information may come and go. Although having no intention at this level can feel very comfortable, your consciousness has become scattered. Go to an ever more subtle level with a light yet focused intention, until you come to no thoughts.

"The Middle Way" — in Zhineng Qigong, there are a lot of expressions like "observe but not observe," "breathing but not breathing," "empty but not empty," "do but do not do." They all express "The Middle Way." Find this middle ground, in which there is a gentle hint of an intention for something to happen — "happen but not happen."

Different Kinds of Intention

1. Separated intention — as you observe the external world, your intention is divided (from consciousness).

2. Strong intention — often in the beginning, your intention can be strong and focused. This is necessary, since your consciousness is focused on the external world and therefore divided. The strong intention helps to break old habits. A strong intention brings the heart back to the inner space.

Tension in the head (Upper Dantian) or elsewhere in the body? Sometimes when intentions are too strong, you might experience tension in the head. This kind of intention (with attachments) mobilizes bodily Hun Yuan Qi (HYQ), whose center is in the Lower Dantian. This qi spans the whole body, but when it gathers in the center of the head, the qi feels rough and you might feel a sense of heaviness or a headache. When you learn to relax the intention, this light intention gathers very pure and fine qi into Shenji Palace. Then there is no tension. If there is tension in the Upper Dantian, you can open and merge your consciousness with the universe. The qi, which is too concentrated, will open and the pressure will diminish or disappear.

Similar tension can occur elsewhere in the body if the intention is too strong. This comes from qi that has become blocked as a result of the strong intention.

3. Light intention — a light intention is the way to purify consciousness. With practice, your intention can become lighter. Qi also becomes finer and purer, and you can observe to a purer level. The lighter the intention, the purer the level of observation.

Important: any intention can be a limitation. If you have an intention to do something, you can limit yourself on that thing, especially as you go deeper and purer. The intention can also block us from the True Self — because the intention creates the last division.

"I want to find myself." "I am observing myself." "Where is the True Self?"

All these intentions are separations — that is, the observer and the observed are experienced as separate, almost as if there are two observers ("This observer observes that observer"). So a division still exists in our consciousness, even in the Mingjue state.

Actually, there is just one observer. Because the reference framework has the habit of separation, the conditioned mind thinks the observer must always observe something.

So when you observe the Self at the earlier stages of Mingjue Gongfu, you still feel that the Self is the object of your observation. This is a good starting point, but continue to go deeper, to the next level, where there is no intention.

4. No intention — at some point in your practice, the intention disappears. "I have no desire." "I have no judgments." "I am the observer, the Pure Consciousness, Mingjue. I do not need to observe myself. I just am." This is a state of being, or Yiyuanti state. There is no separation.

At this level, it may be difficult to judge whether it is the real True Self (Yiyuanti state, enlightened state — these are interchangeable phrases). But that is not important. There is no need to judge or wonder or ask these questions. Just remain in this state and focus on relaxing and continuing to be purer and finer.

Questions create blockages for the practice. Questions introduce doubt into the pure state, and suddenly, you can bring yourself back down to a lower level.

In Laozi's *Tao Te Ching* (*The Book of The Way and its Virtue*), he described two states:

1. Wu Wei ("Do Nothing") — there is no intention, so in this state, the practitioner does nothing. Another way to say this is to do without resistance or effort. When you experience this "no intention" state, you are free. You know the unity of the self.

2. Wu Bu Wei ("Do Everything") — after the Wu Wei state, the intentions return, but the intentions are free, without attachment. You can do everything in the state of doing nothing, meaning that you do everything, but internally, it is as though you are doing nothing. Your intentions cannot block your state of pure being.

Wu Wei. Wu Bu Wei

At this enlightened level, there is no separation between you and your intentions, meaning you and your intentions are one. You and your thoughts are one. Intention, thoughts — they are all awakened — without fixations or attachments.

> Do everything in the
> "do nothing" state.

Important: Do not become fixated on reaching enlightenment. **The most important focus is to enjoy life!** And by enjoying your pure Mingjue state, you will naturally improve your gongfu.

Highest Level of Intention

Intention at the highest level is to know and experience the answer to the question:

Who am I?

For thousands of years, people have pondered this question. Many have felt variations on being lost: "I do not know who I am. I am always attached to the material (physical) world, I have a lot of fear and suffering. I need to find out who I am." Deep inside is a strong desire to know.

The answer to this question is very simple:

I am.

The direct experience of this "being" is critical — not just mentally understanding the concept. That is why Mingjue Gongfu includes methods to practice, and not just theories to learn. You can also come into this direct experience of beingness by practicing Mingjue in your daily life.

Once you experience the answer to this central existential question for all human beings, your other questions and problems can resolve — health, emotional, societal — and you can attain freedom.

Maybe there are doubts. Can I really do this? How? **The key is to release the questions and instead, learn and practice.** Hold this intention as the foundation of the practice and live your way into the answer.

> The highest level of purpose in
> Mingjue practice:
> to experience True Self.

Two Levels of Mingjue State

The difference between the two levels of Mingjue state is the intention. This is very subtle but important.

1. Fixed Mingjue — this is the first level of practice, when the observer has the intention to observe and maintain itself. Observe, maintain, observe, maintain…. This kind of practice happens on the rougher (coarser) level of duality. In the earlier stages of gongfu, the practitioner usually needs this intention as a discipline to practice.

2. Natural Mingjue — this is the higher level of Mingjue state. After practicing the fixed Mingjue state for a period of time, Mingjue becomes stronger and more stable. When the power of the information in Mingjue is strong enough, the practitioner reaches this state, where the intention is lighter, freer.

Reflection Questions

Why do you practice? For health? Peace? Happiness? Or for another reason?

Intentions contain deep information. When intentions are clear, they will guide the practice.

THE COLLECTIVE FIELD IN MINGJUE GONGFU

Many students of Zhineng Qigong learn and practice individually. Their health, consciousness, and overall gongfu can become stronger. Their egos, however, are also at risk for becoming stronger. "I want happiness!" "I want healing!" "I am strong!" "I can heal this other person!" These strong intentions can themselves create blockages in flow.

Take a moment to study the logo* of The World Consciousness Community (on the following page). It is important to understand all of the information contained in the logo, as it contains the complete teaching and practice of Mingjue Gongfu.

---

* Logo designed by The World Consciousness Community member Andrea A. Tostado

• The big blue circle symbolizes the universe: the qi universe.

• The tree symbolizes life.

• The heart symbolizes the universal love that creates, nourishes, and grounds the beautiful tree of life.

• The small light in the middle symbolizes the pure awakening consciousness that spreads from the Shenji Palace (an empty space in the center of the head).

• That small light expands into the big circle of light — this is the pure collective consciousness field.

• The tree's qi field also merges with this consciousness field.

• The light merges with the heart — Pure Consciousness is awakening to love.

• Each leaf is a whole, representing every individual raising his/her vibration and resonating in the same light of awakened consciousness.

• Each consciousness is illuminated like a star in the center (Shenji Palace), and it awakens others through the principle of resonance.

The collective consciousness field is an entirety state — a state of oneness comprised of the merging of individual Mingjue consciousnesses. Everyone's Mingjue is one with the Mingjue collective field. It is a true state of "we are one." Mingjue is a cosmic and collective awareness state.

So when you practice as a Mingjue Gongfu student, you don't just practice for your individual self. You practice for the whole collective field — the whole community. When others practice in the field, they also practice for you. Everyone practices with their hearts merged as one. Mingjue is rooted in and nourished by universal love.

This is how to practice the community life.

Note: When individual Mingjue merges with the collective field, Mingjue is difficult to shake up. The consciousness field is strong enough to support anyone and everyone. In the past, it wasn't strong enough — people couldn't experience qi very easily. Now people can experience qi quite readily, and many more are committed to practicing higher levels of consciousness.

> When you practice for yourself,
> you practice for the world.

MINGJUE AND QI

Mingjue is a conscious, high-level form of qi. This is distinct from qi in its "natural state." Mingjue is active. It can send (transmit), receive, process, and organize information. It is the self-aware state.

Mingjue is the master of qi. Mingjue can focus on a specific body part or a specific person or place and bring qi into that place. Where Mingjue goes, qi follows.

Mingjue can "die" on qi. If Mingjue only focuses only on practicing qi, or if Mingjue only focuses on external events and people, then Mingjue can become blocked and lose itself.

Mingjue is nourished by qi — both universal and bodily qi. This is a very important teaching and practice in Zhineng Qigong. Qi nourishes consciousness. Practitioners learn to gather universal qi to nourish Mingjue. Universal qi purifies and clarifies Mingjue. Bodily qi can also nourish Mingjue, when it becomes finer and finer. When the innate qi contained within Mingmen Inner Palace (an energy center anterior to L2-3 of the lumbar spine) becomes very fine, it can also nourish Mingjue.

Mingjue and the Qi Body

In the Pure Consciousness state, students learn to observe the physical body as an invisible form: the "qi body."

Through the five sensory organs, the physical body is experienced as concrete: there are boundaries, there is the flesh and the bones, etc. The five senses cannot go beyond that, so this forms the framework of the body being a physical entity.

Mingjue, however, can penetrate through the form, down into the deep inner space of the body. The body, then is experienced as "empty but not empty," meaning that while it may seem empty, it is not empty space. The space is actually subtle energy (qi).

When Mingjue goes through and observes this deep inner space, the body appears as a qi space. This qi body is concentrated, condensed qi. It is relatively stable.

When Mingjue goes throughout the qi body, its qi and information merge and transform (hunhua) with the qi and information of the body.

Qi has many levels. Mingjue can easily observe the rougher levels of qi. The Gongfu of observation, which naturally becomes finer and finer as qi is observed, leads to the experience of internal emptiness — this is necessary for the Mingjue state. This can be experienced by consciousness going to and resting in the Mingmen Inner Palace (the energy center anterior to L2-3 in the lumbar spine). When the observation is fine enough, you come close to Pure Consciousness.

Mingjue and the Qi Field

Part of Mingjue Gongfu is trusting Mingjue to give good information. This is why students learn to surrender any fear of merging with everyone and everything. Mingjue has the potential to transform and purify the qi field of others. Mingjue can also change the qi fields of different environments. These are important practices.

If Mingjue receives information about someone that indicates a problem, Mingjue can immediately send the information of "Haola!" instead of responding with fear. *Haola* means **"All is well!"**

Some of you might wonder, "Why do I have so many problems when others don't seem to?" "Why am I so sensitive?" Sensitivity is not the issue — fear in the consciousness is.

You do not need to re-create the unpleasant or negative sensations in your body. Your inner space will be fine as long as you remember to open your heart and merge with universe, as well as with the collective consciousness field. Universal love will bring benefit to you and the other person(s). If, however, you do pick up some information and feel it inside your body, you do not need to fear. Trust the power of Mingjue. Give yourself the good information of "Haola!"

This is an expression of big compassion. It is also a way that your gongfu can quickly improve.

> Mingjue is the essence
> and the power
> of the qi field.

ENTIRETY IN QIGONG PRACTICE

An entirety is a complete, autonomous unit formed by the merging and transforming (***hunhua***) of two or more substances. **One entirety can merge with another entirety to form a larger entirety.**

An entirety can also be described as **a state of oneness.**

Examples: an atom is an entirety. As is a cell, a person, a community of people, and the planet.

In qigong, an entirety can exist on levels beyond the physical:

- At the qi level of reality (Qi Entirety)

- At the consciousness level of reality (Mingjue Entirety)

Each level and subunit of an entirety follows the rules of the entirety.

Physical matter is an entirety comprised of form, qi, and information. When one physical entirety (or "thing") merges with another or multiple other entireties, it is integrating at the levels of form, qi, and information.

Information that mobilizes enough energy is the key to forming an entirety.

Hunhua of Universal Qi

Hun means merging. *Hua* means transforming.

In addition to observing everything in the universe as qi — including the vast empty space — Qi Entirety Theory includes observing the *hunhua* movement of universal qi. This means that, through training, students can strengthen their subtle observations: the entire qi universe is always in flow, always changing. Everything merges and transforms with each other. Nothing remains static. New life is always being created in alignment with universal laws.

After observing this reality, practitioners realize that any fixed ideas naturally disappear. The notion of wanting life to always remain the same is an illusion, an impossibility.

Qigong methods are designed to guide the movements of body, energy, and life in a positive direction.

LIFE AS AN ENTIRETY

Qi – consciousness – body: these three levels of reality are always merging together and transforming with each other as an entirety, or state of oneness.

However, as people grow into adulthood, this entirety usually becomes more and more fragmented. This is because the dominant reference framework is one of duality: you and me, humans and nature, good and bad, etc. This is a framework that focuses on the material world, and it is limited. This framework says, "I am me, and you are separate from me."

As it is elaborated much more in detail below, Qi Entirety and Mingjue Entirety are expanded states of oneness. The observer observes the whole universe as qi, as well as his or her body as qi, fluidly merging with universal qi. Everything is continually flowing, one into another. The observer sees and experiences everything as one. This framework says, "I am you and you are me. Humans and nature are one. All humans are one."

> You and I are one.
> All living things are one.
> One is everything.
> Everything is one.

The focus of Mingjue Gongfu practice is to restore the original, complete entirety state. This shift can transform people's lives.

First Entirety: the Whole Individual

This entirety is the recognition that the body, consciousness, and internal qi are one, three levels always merging together — that there is no distinct separation between the physical body, qi, and consciousness. This is a smaller entirety.

Second Entirety: the Universal Individual

This entirety is the recognition that the body, consciousness, and qi are always merging together — *and* that this internal qi is also continuously merging with universal qi. That is, the body's internal qi and universal qi are one. This is a time-space entirety. This is a big entirety.

Relationships Between the Body, Consciousness, and Qi

1. These three are in a continuous state of merging together.

2. Of the three, consciousness is the master of this entirety. Whether people know it or not, they are the master of themselves. At times, it may seem that their bodies or their qi (energy) rule their consciousness. When consciousness is not yet awakened — when consciousness does not yet know itself — it does serve qi and the body. In this state, people become attached to whatever is happening in their bodies and to qi.

3. Wherever consciousness goes, qi follows. Consciousness sends the information, and qi flows to create the change. Consciousness can make qi move and change; it can even change the quality and density of qi. Through practice, consciousness can become an increasingly awakened master. In actuality, consciousness is always the master.

Gong Fu

Three Levels of Entirety

Each of the following three levels of gongfu are different and complementary. Each has its unique benefits.

Ultimately, however, all kinds of practice should come to the 3rd (consciousness) level of practice — because it is through this level of practice that the True Self can be realized. Coming to the True Self is the most important thing in life — for self, for humanity, and for natural world.

This is a revolution for life.

1st Level: Consciousness and Qi Serve the Body

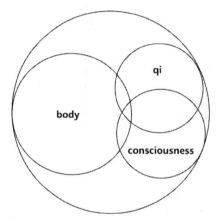

the enirety of qi and consciousness service to body

At this level, the body is the primary focus, and thus the master. Consciousness is always aware that "I am the body" and "Qi is in the body." Both consciousness and qi serve the body.

Example: in martial arts, when a practitioner focuses his consciousness on his muscles and physical strength, and any energy is used for the purpose of improving stamina and physical skill, all of the focus is on the body.

Another example: when practitioners use qigong to enhance their bodies as the primary focus or goal. This is consciousness and qi serving the body; the body is the center of this entirety.

This is a common starting place for students just starting to learn Zhineng Qigong, and there are important benefits to note. With the focus being on the correct posture, form, and movements, their consciousness returns to the interior of their bodies, whereas before this practice, they were only focused on and attached to the external world — how to earn a living, how to relate to other people.

Attachment to the external world creates blockages within the mind and body, and also dissipates energy. Tension, pressure, and fear ensue.

But as soon as consciousness returns to itself — to the physical body — this is already an improvement because energy is gathered inside. By training the body practitioners can still receive benefits.

Potential Pitfalls of the 1st Level of Gongfu:

1. Overtraining — if someone overtrains the body, this can consume energy from within. That is, even though the practitioner doesn't lose energy to the external world, he can still consume too much internal energy.

2. Attachment to the body — when consciousness focuses on the surface of the body, it risks becoming fixated on the body. People may then worry about their bodies: Am I strong enough? Beautiful enough? Healthy enough? Consciousness can then become the slave of the body instead of the master.

2nd Level: Consciousness and the Body Serve Qi

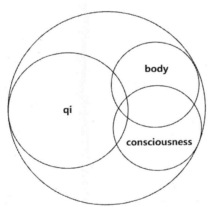

the entirety of body and consciousness service to qi

This is a higher level of gongfu. At this level, the practitioner goes beyond the physical reality, which appears limited and small, and consciousness focuses on the essence of qi.

At this level, consciousness focuses on the body as a qi body. The awareness is not on the muscles or bones or organs of the physical body, but on energy. The form of the body is there, but it is a qi form. This form is full of qi and maintains qi.

There is no inner or outer. Bodily qi therefore connects with the qi of the universe, going beyond the individual, small self. There is a saying in Chinese that captures the Qi Entirety:

TIAN REN HE YI
Humans and the universe are one.

Tian Ren He Yi

By understanding and practicing the Qi Entirety, anyone can learn to:

• Observe the inner qi and the qi of the universe (universal qi)

• Experience the infinite Qi Entirety

• Observe the continuous *hunhua* (merging and transforming) of universal qi

• Experience and observe that change is always happening, that life is change, that every second is new, that each moment creates life anew

With the focus on qi, this state is relaxed. There is no tension or fixation on either the material world or the physical body. The experience goes beyond the five sensory organs and their sensations. The qi universe is empty, a direct experience of the infinite. This creates a very harmonious state where consciousness is open.

When consciousness focuses on qi, qi naturally gathers into the body. Consciousness is connecting with the qi and maintaining it inside. Universal qi naturally nourishes the body, at the levels of qi and form.

Daoists mainly practice at this level: they start from internal qi, then merge internal qi with the universal qi.

Potential Pitfalls of the 2nd Level of Gongfu:

1. Attachment to qi — this is a very good level of practice, but consciousness can lose itself in qi, meaning practitioners can become attached to the blissful and strong feelings of qi.

2. Subconscious fear — even if the consciousness state feels harmonious, at this level there can still be a lot of underlying fear. There is still a fixation on the body or qi.

Dr. Pang regularly taught students to feel their qi bodies, encouraging them to hold a big qi ball in the standing meditation posture and also while walking.

But he also warned them: "Do not die on qi!" Do not focus too strongly on the good qi feeling. This is only part of the process. There is still a third level entirety practice.

3rd Level: Qi and Body Serve Consciousness — Mingjue is the Master

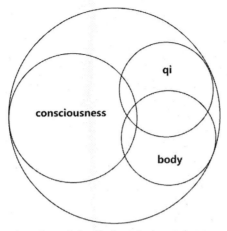

the entirety of qi and body service to consciousness

This is the highest level of qigong practice, where consciousness (Mingjue) is the master. Qi and the body are in service to the awakening, strengthening, and purifying of consciousness.

At this level, the body holds qi internally and this qi goes toward nourishing consciousness. Universal qi also nourishes consciousness. Consciousness, or "the observer," starts to observe any thoughts, emotions, and sensations that arise. Then the observer observes itself — **this is the Mingjue state. Consciousness is awakening to itself.**

At this entirety level, practitioners realize they are not just their physical bodies or their qi bodies. They realize consciousness as the center. "Ah, I am the observer!" The True Self. Consciousness merges with the qi body and the whole qi universe.

> Consciousness is the center.
> Consciousness is the essence.

With a clear, centered, and awakened consciousness, nothing can enslave consciousness anymore. This is a very peaceful, relaxed, and beautiful state. The inner heart is free: it doesn't hold onto anything.

At this level, practitioners can easily:

- Experience a free state of being
- Experience universal, unconditional love

- Draw support from the collective consciousness field
- Come to the state of harmony in consciousness just by thinking of it

From Dr. Pang's book: "In this [high-level entirety] state, the body and qi will move once the mind moves, and the body and qi will be silenced once the mind is silent. Cessation of the breath or the heartbeat through the practice of static meditation is an example of this state, as is the ability to fly in the air at the highest levels of martial arts."

Subtle Difference Between the 2nd and 3rd Levels:

If you are doing a breathing practice, even though you are learning to train your consciousness, this is still mainly a practice at the level of energy or qi. If you become aware, however, of *who* is breathing, and *who* is observing the breath, this is the consciousness level entirety.

Potential Pitfalls of the 3rd Level of Gongfu:

1. **Old conditioned patterns** — this consciousness level practice still contains different reference frameworks within it — old frameworks of thinking and doing that contain fixed ideas and old habits. These will emerge in your daily life when you meet various obstacles and challenges. The important thing is to always remember to connect to the consciousness entirety, so the old mental frameworks do not enslave you. Instead, use the frameworks as tools in a free consciousness state.

2. **Ego pride** — just because some practitioners choose to begin practicing from the 3rd (consciousness) level does not necessarily mean they have a higher level of consciousness. It just means they are practicing the methods of a high level. It is important to continue practicing, observing, and merging with the collective field. This can help to practice and observe with honesty and humility.

MINGJUE ENTIRETY

Mingjue Entirety is a state in which Mingjue merges with the collective consciousness field, then merges with the qi entirety — that is, the emptiness of the qi body, part by part, together with the emptiness of the qi universe.

Mingjue, the self-aware observer, is the center of this infinite entirety. Because **Mingjue makes the universe conscious**, this is **an awakening entirety.**

In the diagram below, Mingjue is the observer in the middle of life and the universe:

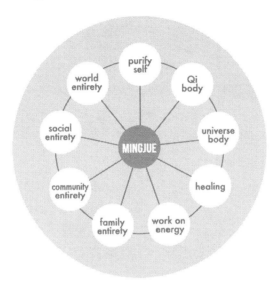

Through Mingjue Gongfu, Mingjue can learn to:

- Transform the physical body into a qi body — and Mingjue merges to fill the qi body

- Merge with universal qi, mobilize universal qi — and Mingjue remains autonomous (and therefore is not fixed by qi)

- Heal yourself and others

- Perceive and generate subtle energy, like electricity and magnetism

- Connect with and transform the "family entirety," recognizing that you and your families are one; Mingjue creates harmony by being present as love, not becoming attached to others

- Connect with the "community entirety," embracing the diversity of thoughts and ideas, staying in Mingjue state to merge with, communicate to, and be present in love toward others, not being blocked by individual fixations or separateness

Mingjue expresses in all social relationships. Relationships in the family, community, and society represent an expansion from a smaller to larger field. All social relationships are expressions of the state of one's consciousness: one's own state together with the state of others. When people communicate with each other in the Mingjue state, the mind's framework is relaxed and free. Without Mingjue consciousness, the ego and duality rule and can easily generate friction.

When you stay in Mingjue state, harmony can come to all your relationships. When you train Mingjue in the "world entirety," you participate in co-creating a harmonious world — for humanity and the natural world (plants, animals, and everything else).

Reflection Questions

These two sets of questions are very important in Mingjue Gongfu:

1. When you move through your life's activities, who is doing those activities? For example, if you listen to music, who is listening to the music? What reactions do you notice?

This question seems very simple, but it is profound. Can you always connect your sensory organs to the inner source? Or do you lose yourself to the experience of the sensory organs?

2. What is the experience when the observer observes itself?

Everyone has an inner observer. When the observer observes itself, what is the rough experience? What is the subtle experience?

Where is the observer? What is the state of the observer?

Mingjue Entirety: Different Centers of the Universe

When an individual Pure Consciousness merges with the collective consciousness field and universal qi, it forms the Mingjue entirety. In qigong, there are different ways practitioners can apply Mingjue entirety to the practice methods.

Over time, Mingjue practitioners become aware that **they are the center of their own qi universe.** Depending on where their consciousness chooses to focus, there are different centers within the body:

- The Lower, Middle, or Upper Dantian serve as the center of universe.

- The Middle Channel serves as the center of universe — the experience is that the Middle Channel has no boundaries, that it is the center of universe and the Middle Channel is one with universe.

• Humans and the universe are one (*Tian ren he yi*) — for those who can maintain this state of awareness, universal qi will draw into whichever center is the primary focus, and that center becomes the center of their universe, created by the information in their consciousness. Breathing also happens in and from this center. When the center moves (for example, while walking or driving or dancing), the whole qi body is moving, so the qi field and the whole universe move, too. In this state, qi quickly becomes more abundant and clear.

• The centered state of consciousness — in this centered state, there are no attachments; only the present moment. This consciousness state is autonomous, naturally merged with the universe. The consciousness center merges with the center of the body. This creates a conscious, centered life state.

Mingjue-Centered States

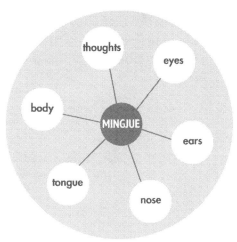

There are four Mingjue-centered states, where the function of Mingjue becomes progressively more expanded:

1. A pure Mingjue state (this is the core) — simply feeling the pure Mingjue state of "empty but not empty," and experiencing it as independent, autonomous.

2. Pure Mingjue with central information (universal love + happiness + gratitude) — whereas a pure Mingjue state is empty, a function of Mingjue is to send good information; so this state forms a Mingjue universal love entirety to create a new life, a new world.

3. A second state of pure Mingjue with central information (loving kindness information that infuses all thoughts, bodily sensations, and the five sensory organs) — Mingjue universal love and happiness permeate throughout the entire body and mind, and throughout all aspects of the practitioner's life.

4. A centered, universal entirety — Mingjue universal love connects with everything, expanding to fill the whole universe.

YIYUANTI THEORY

Yi Yuan Ti

Yiyuanti can be thought of as the highest level of Mingjue consciousness, or an awakening of the True Self. So, to develop Mingjue Gongfu, it is important to have a basic understanding of Yiyuanti Theory.

Mingjue practice is, in fact, based on Yiyuanti Theory — the core and most important dimension of Dr. Pang's Hun Yuan Entirety Theory. After Dr. Pang experienced enlightenment, he developed Yiyuanti Theory to try to describe and explain it for others.

In the two-year masters training at the Huaxia Center ("Medicineless Qigong Hospital") in China, Dr. Pang taught the students to realize two fundamental theories and experiences:

1. Universal or Original Hun Yuan Qi (the Source of the creation of the universe)

2. Yiyuanti (the inner master, the internal essence of humans — the Source of the creation of human consciousness)

When these two experiences merge together, human consciousness joins the universe's creation at a very high level.

Most spiritual traditions describe an enlightenment state. Similarly, Yiyuanti Theory can help people attain enlightenment and come to know, through experience and awareness, the answer to the essential question, "Who am I?"

Q: Who experiences Yiyuanti?

A: Yiyuanti experiences itself. This is what enlightenment means.

WHAT IS YIYUANTI?

According to the Three Layers of Matter Theory (described in subsequent sections), everything has three levels of existence: physical (material) – energy – information. These three levels are always merging together as an entirety.

As human beings, there is a physical body, the energy inside and around the body, and the information of that energy — the energy inside the body and also the energy of the whole universal space around it.

It is the same for brain cells. Each brain cell has its own energy and energy field, and each brain cell contains its information. **Yiyuanti is a very fine, pure level of qi and the information field contained by the brain cells**.

Brain cells are qi that has condensed and manifested in physical form. The invisible (or formless) qi is flowing throughout the brain cells.

Two Kinds of Invisible Qi Flow Within Brain Cells:

1. Qi at the energy level — this is like the electronic waves inside and around the brain, like electricity in and around cables or wires.

2. Qi at the information level — this a very pure kind of qi. The pure qi of the brain cells and the pure qi of its information merge together and connect with the pure qi of the body's entire central nervous system. At this level, the qi is very special — it has gone beyond the physical time-space dimension and beyond "ordinary thought." Some say that this energy is manifesting in another dimension, in a different time-space state. This energy occupies the brain cells as well as the emptiness of the universe. It is everywhere and in everything, in the past, in the future. There is no time. Yiyuanti is such an existence — it is the pure qi of information.

Relationship of Yiyuanti, Consciousness, and Thoughts

This analogy of water and waves may help to explain this more clearly:

If Yiyuanti can be likened to water, then consciousness is the wave. The wave can take on many forms, including thoughts, but in essence, all the waves are water. It cannot be said, however, that water is the wave(s). Water is just water.

When you are only aware of different thoughts, it is as if you are only aware that the waves are waves (and not water).

If you become aware that all different kinds of waves are in essence water, you can come to Yiyuanti. The waves are forms, but through the forms you see the True Self. When you practice Mingjue at a certain level, you come to experience that your **True Self is within your thoughts; and your thoughts are the movement of the True Self. There is no separation. Thoughts and Yiyuanti are one.** This is highest level of the inner consciousness entirety (or the highest level of Mingjue).

Q: Where do thoughts come from?

A: From the movement of Yiyuanti with information.

Relationship Between Yiyuanti and Mingjue

At the beginning, the practice focuses simply on observation — this is the Mingjue level. It's called "Mingjue" because Yiyuanti hasn't fully realized itself yet. Self observing self is happening at a lower, rougher level. And the fixed reference framework (ego mind) is still a strong habit.

When Mingjue reaches the awareness of Yiyuanti, the experience is very clear, like a mirror wiped clean of all the dust and grime that had accumulated since childhood. "Ah, I am Yiyuanti."

Teacher Wei: "Your life will transform beyond your wildest imagination. But do not try to imagine what enlightenment might be like — these imaginings can become blockages."

Three Levels of Yiyuanti in Consciousness

1. Knowledge of Yiyuanti theory

2. Visualization of Yiyuanti — at this level, the student knows the characteristics of Yiyuanti from the theory and can naturally visualize this state. This is similar to visualizing the blue sky when someone says, "Close your eyes and see the blue sky." The image of the sky immediately comes to your mind. Or if someone says, "emptiness," the mind instantly experiences emptiness.

3. True state of Yiyuanti — at this level, the student experiences the reality of Yiyuanti (or True Self or enlightenment). This level is a state of being, meaning that no one can conceptualize or visualize this level.

CHARACTERISTICS OF YIYUANTI

1. Yiyuanti is Pure Equilibrium

Yiyuanti is very even, pure, subtle and fine. The state of Yiyuanti is the same everywhere. There is no difference in its qualities in the inner space of the head, in and around the body, in the mountains, the ocean, or in the earth. It is very even and pure, like emptiness itself.

Yiyuanti state is similar to the Original Hun Yuan Qi of the universe.

In the beginning, students can start by visualizing Yiyuanti's purity. The process of visualization can help to observe greater and greater levels of purity. However, this visualization is real (not just imagined), and it can guide students to observe an ever deepening level of reality.

2. Yiyuanti Reflects Everything

Yiyuanti, or the pure qi of brain cells, is like an infinite, invisible mirror that reflects everything. Most importantly, this mirror can reflect itself.

Using the metaphor of a physical mirror, it is easy to understand that the mirror reflects things outside of itself. Likewise, the invisible mirror of Yiyuanti can also reflect things outside of itself. But Yiyuanti also has the unique ability to reflect itself, and when it does, this state is called "enlightenment."

Yiyuanti (the mirror) is totally clear and pure. So in Mingjue Gongfu, when the practices focus on "purifying and clarifying Yiyuanti," it is actually the purification and clarification of the smudges. The smudges represent the attachments and fixations of the ego ("the reference framework") that distorts the clarity of Yiyuanti.

3. Yiyuanti Actively Gathers and Disperses

Yiyuanti has the functions to open/gather and close/disperse. It can also choose something and direct its focus there. When Yiyuanti has a single focus, Yiyuanti gathers the qi of all the different levels (Original Hun Yuan Qi, the Hun Yuan Qi of everything, human Hun Yuan Qi, and consciousness Hun Yuan Qi) into that place); then it opens and disperses all different levels of qi. Yiyuanti is the "master of the universe."

4. Yiyuanti Has an Unintentional Movement

This movement of Yiyuanti goes beyond the speed of light. For example, if someone suddenly connects with the sun, his Yiyuanti is focused on the sun and therefore receives the information of the sun. It is the same with sending information. For example, if you send good information to someone, even across a big distance, if you have the information in your Yiyuanti, the information will affect the receiver.

This can also be called the passive or unconscious movement of Yiyuanti.

5. Yiyuanti has an Intentional Movement

This movement can be slower or faster than the speed of light — it is controlled.

For Yiyuanti itself, there is no difference between passive and active movement. All of Yiyuanti's movements are just the process of Yiyuanti working on information — receiving, sending, and processing — as the master.

This can also be called the active or conscious movement of Yiyuanti.

State of Yiyuanti

Q: What is the state of Yiyuanti? Is it like nothingness?

All humans have the original memory of Yiyuanti and know the experience of it, even if most with "ordinary consciousness" cannot remember it.

The following information comes from Yiyuanti Theory:

During the fifth and seventh months of fetal development, the pure qi of the brain cells is ready to merge together and form a special qi entirety; this entirety, which has the potential to develop into conceptual thinking, is called Yiyuanti.

When Yiyuanti appears — and at the moment that Yiyuanti reflects itself — this is the True Self. This is a natural state of being, a natural function of doing or expressing. It is also called the "pure baby heart" state. There is no intention of reflecting or trying to reflect itself or anything else.

The very first function of Yiyuanti is reflecting itself; this happens instantaneously. Then it begins to reflect increasingly more external information. For example, the mother's body, the environment, the universe. As more information — and stronger information — floods the body of the fetus, this information merges with Yiyuanti and begins to overshadow the pure information of the True Self.

So while the original pure memory of Yiyuanti remains, other information overshadows it. At and after the moment of birth, babies receive even more information through the five sensory organs. The external information grows stronger and stronger, gradually causing most to forget the True Self.

When consciousness chooses to return to its pure origin, the memory of the original Yiyuanti begins to appear.

Observe. Visualize. Experience.

Functions of Yiyuanti

The functions of Yiyuanti can provide guidance to return to Yiyuanti. In Mingjue Gongfu, students learn first and foremost to apply the functions of Yiyuanti to return to itself, rather than applying them to the external world.

1. Yiyuanti receives information — normal and paranormal.

Yiyuanti receives "normal" or ordinary information through the five sensory organs. Everyone knows how to receive this kind of information. In general, humans can see, hear, smell, taste, and touch.

When you see something, for example, it's important that you recognize this function comes from Yiyuanti — that Yiyuanti exists within you. If you only relate the sense of sight to the colors and forms of objects as seen with the physical eyes, you can easily lose the self.

By recognizing Yiyuanti as the master when you see something, you can realize, "I am pure, clear, and peaceful on the inside. The mirror within me reflects light, color, and form, and therefore I can see." If you can shift to this perspective and inner experience, you can become very centered.

You can also attain enlightenment through the function of the sensory organs — like the Compassionate Buddha, who became enlightened by listening to the sounds of the ocean waves and realizing there was a Pure Consciousness reflecting the sounds to him.

Yiyuanti receives paranormal information. Paranormal ability is when Yiyuanti knows something directly, without receiving information through the five senses. The information can be an image or an auditory signal, too. Yiyuanti can receive information from very long distances away, transcending time and space (paranormal abilities are explained in greater detail in the section "Super Abilities").

Example: if someone suddenly knows someone else's internal state — harmonized or distracted — that is Yiyuanti directly reflecting information.

2. Yiyuanti processes, saves, and retrieves information.

Yiyuanti stores all the information it receives, like a computer database. All information merges and transforms together within Yiyuanti. Then Yiyuanti processes this information and generates new information. This is how new creative ideas emerge.

Yiyuanti can also remember and retrieve information. When particular information is needed, that information can suddenly be retrieved. For example, if someone asks, "What is DNA," Yiyuanti retrieves the information about DNA and also other related information.

3. Yiyuanti sends information — normal and paranormal.

Sending information is a very important function of Yiyuanti. When people communicate, teach, sing, and laugh, Yiyuanti is sending specific information. Modern science and other academic disciplines are also created by sending ordinary information through the five senses.

Yiyuanti can also send paranormal information. Yiyuanti does not need the body, the senses, or input from any kind of artificial intelligence. Yiyuanti directly sends information.

Mingjue healing is an example of Yiyuanti sending paranormal information — the information goes beyond the five senses. There are no concepts or sensations. Just a pure intention.

Important: Applying Yiyuanti Theory to this, the practice of observation is considered a form of receiving information, and Yiyuanti reflects what it observes.

When Yiyuanti receives information from itself — meaning the observer observes itself — this is the Mingjue state. Alternatively, one can say that, when the pure mirror of Yiyuanti reflects itself and clearly knows itself, this pure state is the Mingjue state.

REFERENCE FRAMEWORKS

What is a Reference Framework?

It is any standard, pattern, or inner program by which the mind judges, analyzes, and perceives things. Reference frameworks are within the dualistic world — the world of "form." Everything is relative and comparative.

More simply stated, the reference framework is a system formed by information that is reflected in Mingjue (some conscious, some unconscious).

The reference framework helps people to understand:

- How the process of thinking works
- Where judgment and perspectives on experiences come from
- How the material world and its systems operate

Reference frameworks are not in and of themselves problematic or negative. If understood and applied in a free consciousness state, reference frameworks are tools for anyone to navigate the material world. Pure Consciousness can create different lifestyles and philosophies based on different reference frameworks.

Deep inside each person, there is a standard through which he comes to judge what he encounters in the world. For example, height and weight. The reference framework is like a computer program that guides people in judging "good" versus "bad."

Reference frameworks explained by Yiyuanti Theory: after Yiyuanti receives information, this information stays within Yiyuanti and connects with all the other information inside Yiyuanti, continually building a reference framework.

While the reference framework builds the patterns for a dualistic world, this dualistic world exists within oneness — in the entirety. The yin-yang symbol can help us understand how duality and oneness coexist in one entirety.

The circle represents the infinite entirety. It is the symbol of the entire time-space totality.

However, within the circle, there is duality — this is the reference framework. The two colors (black and white) represent negative and positive. Calling one side "black" or "yin" or "negative," and the other side "white" or "yang" or "positive" is an example of judgment. When someone lives and perceives his life from within this level, he is limited to the reference frameworks. When he say things like, "You are right," or "You are wrong," he actually means, "Your reference framework is right," or "Your reference framework is wrong."

Important: Do not overlook that, for the yin-yang symbol, the black also contains a small white dot, and vice versa. Positive and negative are in each other, and they also come together to form a state of oneness. When someone lives from beyond the duality, that is an entirety state.

In Zhineng Qigong, the focus of the practices is mainly at the entirety level. The entirety level includes the principles and complementary forces of yin and yang, even as the focus remains on the entirety or whole.

In the Mingjue state, students can still perceive and experience life at the duality level, but without losing the entirety state.

Dr. Pang: a Teaching of Duality

People living in the world often have two seemingly opposing dimensions: (1) their desires and (2) wanting to avoid the suffering that often comes with those desires.

Dr. Pang described this dilemma with a metaphor. It's like we're afloat in the ocean, he said, with our feet standing on two different boats. One foot stands in the boat of desires, the other foot in the boat moving toward freedom. We want both. As we set off into the ocean, it is still possible to stand in both. But as we go deeper and deeper into the ocean, if we're still standing on two separate boats, we will fall into the ocean.

To go deeper into the ocean (to practice at higher levels of Mingjue), the ego has to choose one and surrender the other. We have to give up our foot in the boat of desires and stand firmly in the boat that will bring us toward the shore of freedom — to the True Self. On the path to this other shore, we may feel wobbly standing on one boat or the other. Or we may feel unsure, moving back and forth, back and forth, between the boats. This is common. Over time, however, we can feel more confident, steady, and relaxed.

A state of freedom doesn't mean we give up everything from our ordinary daily life, no! We still have everything. We still have the physical body. We still eat food and sleep and use our bodies. And we can still enjoy any and all of it.

But we go beyond it, too. We just stay in the peaceful Mingjue state because we know we are the master of our desires, and not the slave. As master, we can manage our sensory organs. This means we still experience pleasure and other sensations. Our Mingjue, however, observes the whole body, keeping centered and stable, while our body remain harmonious and comfortable — no matter what the ocean brings.

FIVE STAGES OF YIYUANTI

The changes of Yiyuanti occur along with the changes of the reference framework. There are five stages of Yiyuanti development:

1. Pure Yiyuanti: the Empty State

Ling Yuan

Yiyuanti first appears — roughly between the fifth and seventh months of fetal development when brain cells undergo a lot of growth and change — because the qi field of the brain cells is strong enough to form Yiyuanti. Yiyuanti in this state is very pure and empty. Yiyuanti receives information about itself and has its original function to reflect itself. This window of time is very short, but it is nonetheless a state of enlightenment. Zhineng Qigong refers to this state as **lingyuan**.

The emergence of the reference framework. Shortly thereafter, Yiyuanti begins to receive information about the body through the nervous system. Feelings of the body begin to appear within

Yiyuanti. These form instincts are the beginning of the reference framework. The sensations of the body appear, life information appears, and the information from the father's body, the mother's body, and the environment quickly introduce themselves within Yiyuanti. This all happens very fast.

Next, information about the larger universe appears within Yiyuanti. The developing fetus contains so much information, acquired through sensory organs and the nervous system, but it is in a **"natural state,"** meaning there is no awareness of this information yet. So there is no conscious access to it.

2. Self Yiyuanti: Natural and Free

At birth, the baby enters the external world. The infant continuously receives more information from the environment: images, sounds, smells, textures, tastes. This repetition strengthens and activates the information within Yiyuanti. It is still quite natural, as logical thinking has not yet developed. "Self Yiyuanti" means consciousness connects with simple information through the sensory organs. It is a natural and free state, in which **thinking largely occurs as images.** There are no fixations; only a simple duality of awareness of what is internal (subjective) and what is external (objective). There is a simple feeling of "self," "me," "my body."

3. Fixed, Distorted Yiyuanti: Attached and Blocked

The child grows. She learns languages. She receives logical information from her parents. She receives information from school, teachers, books, and the Internet. Society introduces a lot of information. At this point, **logical thinking, judgment, and choices develop.**

This level of awareness creates a dualistic reality: white and black, right and wrong, positive and negative. On the positive side, there is a positive reference framework. On the negative side, there is a negative reference framework. The reference framework supports whatever positive or negative state people experience, or whatever judgments they make about what is good or bad. Attachments and expectations develop. Sometimes a negative reference framework fights with a positive one and wins; sometimes it loses. The pattern becomes stronger.

This level of Yiyuanti is called "fixed and distorted." It can cause a lot of suffering.

Many people live their entire lives at this level.

4. Full and Perfect Yiyuanti: Wise and Free

Consciousness seeks more inner freedom. It starts to observe deeper and deeper within and learns to go beyond the conditioned reference framework.

When Mingjue students first come to Mingjue state, they are still in the fixed and distorted reality. Even though the pure, original Yiyuanti is there, the reference framework is still there, and its patterns are strong.

By continuously observing within, deeper and deeper — observing, concentrating, relaxing — students can break the conditioned, fixed and distorted reference framework. The reference framework begins to lessen its influence over the inner observer, and the observer becomes more and more powerful. Pure Mingjue — or Yiyuanti — can be experienced.

Yiyuanti still contains the dualistic framework. It uses the reference framework in a free state to relate to the material world and societal laws. But consciousness is not fixed or controlled by the reference framework — Yiyuanti has the ability to go completely beyond it (like the entirety state of the yin-yang symbol explained earlier). Mingjue students learn to go beyond any information from the body and even transcend instincts.

This is true wisdom.

Reference frameworks in the free state — consciousness can freely choose which reference framework(s) to use. For example, someone can choose a framework of material science or a framework of Zhineng Qigong. Both are examples of reference frameworks.

"No problem!" In this "full and perfect" Yiyuanti stage, this phrase expresses the full and perfect state of consciousness. The world and everything in it is always moving and transforming, is always reflected in the mirror of Yiyuanti. So what is the problem? At this level, Pure Consciousness observes that life is always changing in each moment. "No problem" sends good information to both the sender and the recipient.

5. Hunhua Yiyuanti: Pure Light

In Zhineng Qigong, this is the last stage of Yiyuanti. The body becomes pure light — pure, invisible qi. At this stage, Yiyuanti is fully autonomous, so the body can change into different forms, disappear and reappear, depending on the information that Pure Consciousness sends to the body. This is a very, very high level.

Hun Hua
Merge and Transform

YIYUANTI AND THE REFERENCE FRAMEWORK

As a review, the reference framework is the standard, pattern, or inner program by which the mind judges, analyzes, and perceives things. It includes:

- Societal knowledge systems (politics, religion, laws, education, medicine, etc.)
- The human body
- The sensory organs and sensations
- The complete material (physical) world

The Mistaken Self — Fixated on the Reference Framework

Many people mistakenly believe that they are their reference frameworks; they therefore become fixated on them. Identities in society are a good example ("I am a teacher," "I am a gardener," "I am a baker."). This happens because people do not know that, beyond their identities and the organizational systems, they are Yiyuanti.

The "ego mind" is another phrase for the "mistaken self" because it is fused with the rigid reference framework. If life circumstances align with their reference framework, the ego can feel very powerful. If the circumstances do not readily align with the reference framework, the ego can feel limited.

The Lost Self — Lost Within the Reference Framework

If the reference framework is very strong, and Yiyuanti (True Self) is therefore hidden (the clear mirror hidden behind the smudges), people can easily lose themselves to their belief systems and thoughts, as well as to the external world. They can feel very lost, especially when their reference framework no longer works for their lives. The essential question, "Who am I?" becomes a big confusion.

Yiyuanti is the Master, the Reference Framework is its Tool

In Yiyuanti, **there is no "right" or "wrong"** — **just *different*.** Everyone's thoughts are everyone else's thoughts. They are all equal. Nothing feels more important or special than something else.

When you arrive at Yiyuanti, everything in your life is reflected in this harmonious state of oneness. Yiyuanti can still use the reference framework to engage in logical, analytical thinking. But consciousness is no longer enslaved or trapped by it.

When you practice Mingjue, you train to observe, observe, observe. Don't think. **Mingjue is an observation practice**, not a mind practice. If you think, you will begin to judge, and that comes from the reference framework. When you observe, you begin to use the function of Yiyuanti, and this takes you ever closer to the True Self.

Reference Frameworks in Daily Life

When Yiyuanti uses reference frameworks as a tool, Yiyuanti can create and choose different lifestyles. This includes thoughts, codes of conduct, health, relationships, emotions, and practices.

Thoughts: Thoughts are expressions of the reference framework and the information contained within Yiyuanti — meaning that thoughts come from Mingjue using information. Put another way, Mingjue is the being of thoughts.

Lifestyles and Codes of Conduct: Why do different people have different lifestyles and habits? Why do people have different reactions to the same events?

A: People have different internal programs (reference frameworks) based on their life experiences. They have different understanding, behaviors, and personalities. Most often, people make judgments based on the framework, and in this sense, the framework is what makes these choices.

When you can see that everyone has different reference frameworks, and that this is why there are different opinions and reactions, you can more easily accept others' differences. You become aware that the internal program (reference framework) is what is deciding all these phenomena.

Health

If someone receives a lot of positive information from early in childhood and her reference framework as an adult contains positive and harmonious information, this can lead to a positive outcome. This can naturally affect her lifestyles and behavior, too, which affects her energy and health.

If the opposite is true, if someone receives a lot of difficult information — like trauma — this can lead to a negative impact on health and behavior.

These are general patterns. Every situation and person are different, and many do not fit this pattern. Sometimes, powerful information can overwhelm the other (previous) information and lead someone's life in new direction. A very positive person can grow up in a very negative family. Information might fixate people to one side, or might push others to another side. Especially when someone is starting to consciously practice Mingjue, negative life experiences can become a gift that helps her see through her life and go beyond these experiences.

A New Reference Framework: Qi and Mingjue

The more the qi and Mingjue framework is in one's consciousness, the more this information will integrate and form a powerful **qigong reference framework**. This qigong reference framework is different from the old reference frameworks and patterns. A qigong reference framework will lead to qigong thoughts and thinking.

The most important thing is to have a **qigong life state**. Qigong provides a framework to study and directly experience the laws of life and the universe. The system of knowledge of qigong is founded upon the science of life and consciousness. This system can teach people to apply this science to live their lives.

It is similar to learning to use any other tool, like cell phones or computers. If you do not learn, you will not know how to use them.

Mingjue reference framework is different from other reference frameworks. The experience of Mingjue transforms all other reference frameworks so that they always support the development or maintenance of the Mingjue state.

In this practice, there is a new reference framework: **everything is possible.** This one sentence can help break through and transform any limiting patterns. Mingjue can break the old, fixed patterns of previous reference frameworks and build a new one based on the following:

- A new, harmonious entirety
- Awakening consciousness
- A collective consciousness field
- Universal love

In the new state, the reference framework is continuously upgraded by studying Hun Yuan Entirety Theory, practicing qigong and Mingjue methods, having new life experiences, and using new abilities and wisdom to serve the greater community and world.

Beyond Theory into Direct Experience

For qigong and Mingjue reference frameworks to serve as guides for life, they must take a strong and central position in the reference framework. **There must be great trust in them.**

For example, according to the Entirety Theory, everything is qi, including the body. This theory is very simple, but consciousness must change to accept this as reality. The shift in consciousness comes from a direct experience of qi. The shift in awareness is, "I am qi," and "I am the observer observing myself."

These direct experiences, in turn, strengthen the reference frameworks in qigong and Mingjue consciousness state — a self-reinforcing cycle.

Reviewing the Information Again and Again

The inner programming needs to gain power to be fully integrated and for gongfu to deepen and advance. Zhineng Qigong theories and practices can be reviewed again and again. Practice throughout your daily lives!

Making Decisions: Old or New Reference Framework?

The old reference framework is used to making life decisions. So how do you make the best decisions from the new qigong and Mingjue reference framework?

1. First, come to a good Mingjue entirety state and go beyond the old reference framework.

2. Study Zhineng Qigong theories and Hun Yuan Entirety Theory. Learn about the laws of the universe, human life, and society. Gradually, make Zhineng Qigong theories and Hun Yuan Entirety Theory the central information in your reference framework. This body of knowledge springs forth from explorations on how to create a better life and world together.

3. Practice using the qigong and Mingjue reference framework to make decisions in your life. What is good for my life? What is good for my relationships? In answering these questions, apply the new reference framework. This can give you new direction and also strengthen the new reference framework at the same time.

4. The Zhineng Qigong standard of human life is called Daode Theory (see more details in a subsequent section). This theory states that, if something is good for the self but not good for others, do not choose this option; do not cause problems for others. Wisdom is finding a way to benefit yourself and others at the same time. Other potential questions: What is good for the entirety? What is good for the greater public? "The greater good" is an important measure because it may not be possible, especially in urgent situations, to find a completely harmonious choice.

5. For personal choices, you — and only you — can change the information for yourself. The basic guideline is to consider the entirety (or whole). The task of making decisions requires both wisdom and flexibility. When you come to the Mingjue state, decisions come naturally, and often these questions will not arise.

Following the Wisdom of the Inner Guide for Life's Challenges

When challenges and suffering come to your life:

1. Do not mind the suffering — this is the way of true wisdom. When you confront any source of suffering, you can choose to respond by coming directly to the inner observer — to pure Mingjue — and remain there. You are the observer observing the suffering, but you do not get entangled with it. You can observe the inner observer and also merge into the collective consciousness field, merging into the universe's pure and infinite qi and surrendering to this conscious universal entirety. Surrender, surrender, surrender…. Experience complete relaxation inside your heart. Release the struggle. Release the resistance. You are the universe. This entirety has the potential to harmonize all external conflicts and internal challenges within the body. This entirety enables you to be present and respond to the situation with unconditional love instead of projecting your own fear and anxiety into it.

2. Observe the suffering and focus on nothing else — another option is to respond by observing the suffering and relaxing into it. The observer observes or faces the suffering. When you truly observe it in the present moment — when you can merge with the suffering, harmonize with the suffering, and accept the suffering — it will gradually disappear. This is because there is no analyzing or judging of the suffering. You just become a harmonized entirety with it, bringing the good information of the qi and collective consciousness field to merge with it. So harmony and unity naturally emerge.

3. Observe the suffering and go to the root of it — a third option is to see the root of the suffering as arising from old, limited reference frameworks — that the experience of suffering comes from attachments and fixations. The suffering may not entirely disappear, but you can understand the factors that create suffering. You come to accept it and fixate less on it. Based on this understanding, you can begin to change the reference framework in a positive direction — to become more open and flexible. Based on this experience, it can become easier to come to the observer and merge with the entirety again.

Managing Mingjue and Thoughts in Daily Life

Thoughts begin with waking up and continue to mount throughout the day. Thoughts are also active during sleep, appearing unconsciously in dreams. It is only in the Mingjue state that the thoughts begin to diminish and even stop for a while.

So, how can you manage Mingjue and your thoughts?

In the following phrases, "positive" can be likened to the coherent state of energy and consciousness. "Coherent" in these terms refers to being in a state of harmony and flow, like a smooth and regular wave pattern.

1. Zheng nian — positive thoughts

Zheng Nian

Accept whatever thoughts emerge and know that all thoughts are happening within Mingjue. Do not get attached to them; simply observe. If you stay in the Mingjue state, there are no distractions. Mingjue is very clear and calm. Thoughts appear and disappear without resistance because the internal state is peaceful. It is only when you lose the Mingjue state that you follow your thoughts, become attached to them, and allow them to distract you away from the Mingjue-centered state. Over time, it will become easier and easier to stop your thoughts altogether in Mingjue state.

The Chinese words *zheng nian* are important because they can help you manage your thoughts. Mingjue state and positive thoughts are in Mingjue. Both constitute *zheng nian*.

Zheng Qi

2. Zheng qi — positive qi state

The Mingjue state transforms the qi of your body into a positive state. When you have positive qi, this qi creates a particular feeling: *ding tian li di*. That is, your energy body connects to heaven (the formless dimension) and earth (the dimension of form) as you stand upright. Your energy becomes very centered, brave, and harmonious.

Zheng Xing

3. Zheng xing — positive action and behavior

Mingjue positive state and positive qi lead to positive action and positive behavior. In recent years, Dr. Pang has emphasized these three phrases many times.

Bao Ren

4. Bao ren — maintaining a pure Mingjue state

By maintaining a pure Mingjue state, you do not lose yourself on external information or events.

5. Hu nian — protecting and maintaining right thoughts (triggers serve as a test)

Protect and maintain right thoughts. This means when you face various challenges or triggers, you can remain in the universal love state. When somebody says, "I hate you," your Mingjue universal love still says or thinks, "I love you," and remains peaceful.

Hu Nian

The information of hatred can be very strong; it can block and consume qi, and generate toxins in the body.

In contrast, universal love nourishes life, connecting you with the creation of the universe, with the creation of life. You remain in Mingjue state so when others intentionally or unintentionally provoke you, Mingjue love and compassion protect this state and your thoughts. You can see through their words and allow Mingjue love to bring the other person to a more harmonious state within and to recover his baby heart.

6. Zhuan nian — a change or turning of mind, negative habits, and character distortions

Zhuan Nian

It is easy to slip back into former negative habits and follow the distorted, fixed character. Self-awareness is necessary to recognize old patterns and return to Mingjue. Dr. Pang called this recognition of old patterns "catching the inner thief." His advice: when you find an inner thief, aim to catch it in Mingjue state, then observe it disappear. Find these internal negative habits and thoughts and catch them. Find the thief in the act, and do not let it continue causing trouble. At the very moment you catch it, you have already come to Mingjue; because you have gone beyond the thief.

This requires gongfu so the old habits don't control you. This change is often difficult. Sometimes painful. But the more you practice, the more powerful you become in Mingjue.

The challenges in your daily life can serve as regular practice. Repeatedly "catch the thief" as you live your life. Start with small challenges or small habits that no longer serve your highest purpose, and gradually move on to larger ones.

7. Zhong he — a centered, harmonious life state; living in a happy, easy state

If you can effectively transform your thoughts and come back to Mingjue, you will arrive at the centered, harmonious entirety state. A new life naturally appears, contented and easy.

Zhong He

Two Simple Practices for Daily Life:

1. Time in nature — an easy and powerful way to practice in the Mingjue entirety state is to spend time in nature — gardening, working in nature, or walking. Natural settings are an ideal place to experience the Mingjue Entirety and transformation of the qi of the natural world. Allow the Mingjue theories and practice methods to transform your experience with nature. See for yourself: can you experience merging with nature — the soil, the trees, mountains, blue sky, clouds?

2. Communicating with others — usually, communicating with others involves thinking, analyzing, and judging. But communicating in a good Mingjue state can transform that experience because it is a practice of observing. See for yourself: can your Mingjue go beyond the ego-level thinking and judging as you talk with your family member or friend? Can you experience the pure inner master as you engage with others?

DAODE THEORY:
MANIFESTATIONS OF QI

Daode

Daode (sometimes spelled Tao Te, as in *Tao Te Ching*, or *The Book of The Way and Its Virtue*) refers to the different manifestations or existence of Hun Yuan Qi and their functions. Put another way, Daode is the expression and laws of Hun Yuan Qi, together with its movement and transformation.

Example: a tree manifests its Hun Yuan Qi (its form, energy, and the information it contains) and its functions (like photosynthesis, shade, wildlife support, soil cultivation, shelter). Daode is both of these together.

Daode practice is a consciousness or Mingjue level practice; it is focused on changing the internal programming.

FOUR LEVELS OF DAODE

1. Natural Daode — this refers to the manifestations of Original Hun Yuan Qi in the universe and its function

Natural Daode of Humans — when a sperm and egg come together, the Natural Daode of the human begins. The qi of the fertilized egg and its function grow into the developing fetus, expressing the Natural Daode of humans. "Consciousness character" has not yet appeared. As babies grow into adults — even as consciousness character, or Social Daode, develops — their cells still retain Natural Daode.

In Natural Daode, the laws are about balance. If it's too hot, you may choose to wear less clothes. If it's too cold, you wear more clothes. Nature works this way, too. Humans can form a natural harmony with the natural world.

If humans stress the natural balance and destroy the natural world, the natural world will be stressful for human life.

2. Social Daode — this includes the rules and standards of thinking and relating (including social behaviors) between people. The movement of Hun Yuan Qi manifests in human consciousness and includes the various reference frameworks of different cultures.

3. Natural-Social Daode — this is the special life state of an infant, in which there is no distinction between self and others. It is simple, true, and pure — the "baby heart" state with no worries, hatred, or complaints, the state before society's frameworks influence the infant or child and before fixations can take a strong hold. This state usually exists in children three years old and younger. While this is a beautiful state, it is not yet mature. The ability of this level is not high or developed.

4. Social Free Daode — this is the high-level Daode of humanity. In this state, we are free (hence Social Free Daode) and still functioning and relating within society. Through practice, we become selfless, transcend emotions and the fixations of the reference framework, develop super abilities, consciously create a harmonious entirety in our relationships with everyone and everything. These are high-level relationships between humans, and between humans and nature.

Social Free Daode contains all the elements of the other three types of Daode.

At the level of Social Free Daode:

- You live at the highest human potential
- Reference frameworks cannot control you

- Qi is always flowing freely

- The baby heart state is still accessible, as are the natural states and the social frameworks — but they manifest from the highest level of awareness, wisdom, and abilities. **The baby heart has awoken and become self-aware. Life and qigong practice become playful.**

Note: In the first three levels of Daode, you don't fully know who you are yet. Many people can develop super abilities (or paranormal abilities, extrasensory perception) at the Social Daode level, but they are applying these super abilities within a fixed framework.

A Word on "Good" and "Bad"

In Daode Theory, "good" means beneficial to us and also for others. If something is only good for us but bad for others, that is not "good." When something is good, information flows freely. There are no blockages.

> Wisdom is knowing which words
> are good for life,
> for ourselves, and others.
> We choose our words carefully.

The Four Daode Requirements for Zhineng Qigong Practitioners

1. Harmony — the entire order of health. In society, you merge the benefits for yourself with those of others. You go beyond the ego, merge into the group, and bring benefits to the whole.

Example: Teacher Wei's reference framework is in ours; our reference framework is also in Teacher Wei's. Everyone's framework merges together. There is no "good" or "bad" information — it's just the totality of all the information that is. However, everyone has the choice of which information to use to co-create a better life and more harmonized world. The information we choose gathers qi and makes the transformation.

2. Happiness, joy — unconditional happiness, independent of external circumstances. This naturally leads to kindness. When your heart and mind have no blockages or attachments, they are naturally in a free state — this is what we call "happiness," which reflects an internal vitality and flexibility.

3. Natural state — a true and unmasked free state. There are no blockages in your consciousness or qi, especially when you are relating within and to society. You use the reference framework to communicate with others, but maintain Mingjue openness and compassion — a sense of oneness.

4. Dignity — an open state, good body posture, good energy, good entirety state. You are graceful, centered, respectful, and kind.

HUMAN DAODE

Human Daode is the existence or manifestation of Hun Yuan Qi in humans and its function.

- Hun Yuan Qi always works in conjunction with its function.
- Human Daode manifests on different levels.
- Consciousness has to merge with the universe (*tian ren he yi*, or "humans and the universe are one"). It does not serve humanity to separate from or fight against the universe.
- When consciousness resists the flow of universal qi, the energy becomes distorted and agitated (inharmonious).
- When humans live and act in accordance with universal qi, this qi serves as nourishment.

Consciousness Level Daode: When Daode function comes to human consciousness, your consciousness works in accordance with the laws of the universe.

Social Level Daode: When the universe's laws manifest at the societal level.

MINGJUE LOVE

The Mingjue Entirety state is unconditional love. This love is everywhere. It just is — there is no fixed direction and form, and no object. So unconditional love can manifest itself on different things, following the information that is received. It is a state that naturally flows from the Mingjue Entirety state.

Mingjue Love Mantra

I am (we are) Mingjue love.
I am (we are) Mingjue peace.
I am (we are) Mingjue happiness.
I am (we are) Mingjue gratitude.

This is a simple but powerful mantra. Each line helps to create a new time-space structure in your life and release blockages. This mantra can also draw your consciousness back to yourself in the present moment. When you repeat this, you begin to realize that you can completely enjoy your life now: **you do not need to mind anything else.**

Repeat the mantra a few times to yourself.

You may begin to realize that everyone — including you — has this one precious life in this world. Sometimes it is not so easy, but it is yours. Each of us has the opportunity to take care of our one life, to love this life. As we do, life becomes more beautiful. In turn, we bring more beautiful information to the world. When we enjoy our consciousness in the present moment, we have arrived at total acceptance and love of ourselves. We can feel, "Yes, I am beautiful! We are all beautiful!"

This is the purpose of Mingjue Gongfu.

Conditional Love: Love in the ordinary (or dualistic) reference framework is a conditional kind of love. This includes instinctual love at the animal level, including a mother's fierce love for her baby. In this framework, there is often difficulty, resistance, and conflict, because there is always separateness between "you" and "me."

When we experience emotions, we must quickly recognize that these arise from the body and ego. The body and reference framework are tools that our consciousness can observe and use; they are not our master. The practice is to always return to the collective consciousness field, which is Mingjue love.

Characteristics of Mingjue Love

- It is everywhere, it has no boundaries. There is no object, direction, or form.

- This universal love is combined with universal wisdom.

- Mingjue Love is more important than any other condition for our lives.

- This is the beautiful, harmonious state in the present moment.

- It flows through us, enabling us to love everyone, including those we might deem our enemies.

- We can see our intricate and intimate connections and feel deep resonance with others.

At this level, we can use this beautiful consciousness state to observe all the dimensions of our bodies and our lives. We accept ourselves and love ourselves. It is not that we think, "I love myself." Rather, the feelings of love and happiness are naturally expressing in our bodies. Happiness is the natural side-effect when consciousness comes back to itself in the present moment.

In this state, we can enjoy all the wonderful sensations we feel without becoming attached to them. We remain connected to the essence of life — the pure and peaceful consciousness state.

Gradually, with continued practice, the internal state becomes more and more harmonized until there is just one **Mingjue Universal Love Entirety** and nothing else. Everything happens in this awakening universal love entirety. An awakening universal love is the master of this entirety — it manages this entirety.

If you come to this level, life feels beautiful, everything is beautiful, you are full of vitality, and all fear disappears.

Unconditional Love as the Essence of the Universe

Unconditional love expands from the Original Hun Yuan Qi, or Source Energy. This universal love entirety becomes bigger and bigger, merging with and infusing the whole universe, the galaxies, the planets, human society, every individual being and every organic and inorganic thing. We are a conscious, happy, universal love entirety. We are one with everyone and everything.

In this entirety state, everyone's consciousness merges together. This is the highest level of the Mingjue consciousness field. It is the pure, universal, loving hearts merging together, like a worldwide chorus of angels singing in complete harmony.

Universal love is everywhere, including within your Pure Consciousness. Your Pure Consciousness is universal love. It is universal love information received from and sending to the Original Hun Yuan Qi.

A very important thing happens: the big, powerful resonance of this consciousness field appears, and grows in beauty and power. It connects with high-level consciousness states — merging with Dr. Pang's Pure Consciousness and those of all the sages and other enlightened beings. At the same time, this consciousness state merges with and influences the general social human consciousness field.

As someone who is awakening, you are choosing to improve your consciousness and thereby co-cultivating the universal consciousness field. The power of this field supports every individual's Pure Consciousness to become purer and more stable — all of it informed by universal, unconditional love.

MINGJUE LOVE CHANGES SOCIAL DAODE

In the Qi-Consciousness Entirety, each breath brings newness. With each breath, there is renewal of life energy, vitality, harmony and openness.

Social Free Daode happens when we consciously develop our consciousnesses — when Mingjue-level consciousness manifests at the social or societal level.

By focusing at the qi level of gongfu, we can have abundant health, develop super abilities, and also offer healings for others. But at this level, we cannot really transform the quality of our consciousness or that of human society — because we are still working within a dualistic reference framework (an ego level practice), which distorts the Hun Yuan Qi Entirety, or universal state of oneness.

Self-Aware Level of Daode: When Mingjue consciousness starts to recognize itself in all dimensions of life, the quality of consciousness and life improves at a whole new level.

Natural Daode in healthy relationships manifests as connection and intimacy. When Mingjue Love is added to Natural Daode, relationships manifest as freedom and harmony.

One sentence that captures the essence of Daode:

Benefit self, benefit the community.

Q: How can you fully realize this purpose?

A: Connect to the world consciousness field for support. Mingjue love transforms all levels of Daode.

> How much you influence others depends on the strength and stability of your consciousness.

THREE LEVELS OF MATTER THEORY

In Qigong Theory, there are three different levels of matter or reality. In recent years, Zhineng Qigong has used modern science to validate and illuminate this theory. Modern science can now help translate for many people what Zhineng Qigong teachers have experienced directly for a long time.

The following three levels cannot be separated except in concept — because everything contains the three levels at the same time.

Collectively, we can simply call everything "qi."

THREE LEVELS OF MATTER

The following three levels of matter form a unity. This means that everything simultaneously contains these three levels:

1. Material or physical — anything with a form.

This level includes everything we can see and touch, all the way down to things we cannot see or touch but can readily measure, like atomic particles.

Example: the human body, cells, atoms

2. Energy or qi — subatomic particles, the quantum realm

This is a level smaller than atoms, down into the empty space within atoms, to an even finer level of qi — as small as a quantum.

In modern science, the **quantum** is an infinitesimally small particle of energy, and some believe that the quantum is what qigong calls one level of invisible qi.

In qigong, there are many levels qi. Some of these levels are even finer than the quantum. While other levels of qi can transform into a quantum, the quantum can also, in turn, transform into other levels of qi.

3. Information — finer than the quantum, this includes information from nature and from consciousness.

Information is a time-space structure that permeates into all dimensions of reality. It is also noteworthy that everything has a time-space structure, including time and space itself, and this structure is a unity that cannot be separated.

Although qigong calls the information at this level "qi" and qi is often translated as "energy," this information is actually finer than what modern science usually calls energy.

Example: reference frameworks, Mingjue, Yiyuanti, thoughts, and intention.

How the Three Levels Relate

When invisible energy gathers to a certain degree or density, it converts into physical matter. That means that the body and all other physical matter are highly concentrated qi **or energy** that has gathered and condensed into what we experience as form.

As the qi of any form becomes finer and disperses, matter and physical form once again convert back into energy. In other words, atoms disperse to become energy, or qi.

Matter, energy, and information are always one: a unity.

The universe is qi.

The galaxy is qi.

The planet Earth is qi.

All of the natural world is qi.

The Human Body is the Universe

The human body is made of cells, which are made of molecules. Molecules are made of atoms, and atoms are largely empty space. Therefore, we are largely empty space.

The human body is an open system — meaning it is open to the whole universe, merging and transforming (hunhua) with the universe.

Each inner organ's qi space is open to the universe.

Each cell is open to the universe.

Dark Matter

According to modern science, dark matter regularly passes through the human body, colliding with the atoms inside. Dark matter is very fine and travels at high speeds through the universe. When it passes into our bodies, we are not aware of this. Why? Because this level of qi goes beyond the level of electromagnetic waves.

At the level of electromagnetic waves, there is a contraction and an expansion. These two forces — attraction and repulsion — act like a magnet.

Dark matter, however, does not have this characteristic. It goes through the entire body's inner space every second. You can understand this simply as a lot of universal qi passing through the body and, through this movement, the universe is merging with the body.

Seven Movements of Universal Qi

Everything in the universe — which is qi — moves in the following ways. The human body also has these same basic movements.

(1) open and (2) close – between form and formless

(3) out and (4) in – between form and formless (mostly pertaining to form)

(5) gather and (6) disperse – between form and formless

(7) transform – between forms, between form and formless, between formless and formless

Modern science defines these movements as **"breathing."** The entire universe is always opening and closing, or breathing. Plants, animals, humans, and the qi of the body are always opening and closing. Within the body, every cell is always opening and closing.

The movement of "opening and closing" happens in both the form and formless dimensions.

The body's internal qi opens (expands out) and closes (draws in).

In the case of the formless dimension, the density of the qi changes: qi expands (opens) and draws together (closes). It is similar to the method of LaQi (or "Pulling Qi") when we use our hands to open and close the qi ball: the qi between the hands is opening and closing.

"Out and in" applies to both the form and the formless dimensions, but primarily to form.

Internal qi expands out through the surface, and from the surface, it draws inside again.

For the formless dimension — you can visualize the qi field inside a room. In that space, universal qi comes into the qi field, and the small qi field opens back out to the universe.

"Gathering and dispersing" applies to both the form and the formless.

This movement actually occurs together with opening and closing. When the qi gathers, it become denser and converts into form. When qi disperses, the form converts into invisible qi. This movement primarily describes the density of qi: when it gathers, the density increases and becomes form. When the qi disperses, the density decreases and the form becomes qi. This process happens naturally.

Important: Your consciousness can accelerate this natural gathering and dispersing process. This is often experienced in qigong healing techniques. For example, someone's bone can grow back within minutes, or a tumor can disappear in a moment of time. This is high-level consciousness information gathering and dispersing qi at an accelerated speed.

"Transforming" happens in the following ways:

1. Between forms — one form can transform into another form.

2. Between form and formless — like the examples given earlier, when a tumor disappears (form to formless) or a broken bone grows back together (formless to form).

3. Between the formless — different levels of qi can merge with each other and transform.

When you know these movements, you can use your consciousness to practice them movements. A focused and clear mind can engage in opening and closing in a powerful, harmonious, energetically coherent way.

If the qi of your heart opens without blockages, other parts of your heart are also opening in similar fashion. The heart space is very free. When closing, qi draws into all your cells, naturally and harmoniously. The heart is nourished and strengthened. If opening and closing is not complete enough, or its rhythm is disordered or inconsistent, the heart can develop problems. This applies to other parts of your body, too.

MERGE AND TRANSFORM: HUNHUA

Hun means to merge. *Hua* means to transform. *Hunhua* describes a fundamental law of the universe — the movement of qi — which is always merging and transforming.

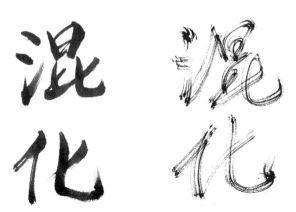

Hun Hua - two styles of calligraphy

If this principle is always in your awareness, you will continually experience renewal. If you face a particular problem, for example, like any health condition, you will always be aware that the situation can quickly change.

Hunhua is always happening.

HUNHUA ACROSS THE THREE LEVELS OF MATTER

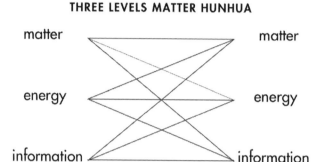

THREE LEVELS MATTER HUNHUA

Matter can transform matter. One material thing can transform with another, combining to form the energy and information of a third thing.

- **Information can transform energy** — information of one material thing can hunhua with its energy. Information and energy are always merging and influencing each other, therefore transforming each other.

- **Energy can transform physical matter** — when physical matter transforms, it also influences its energy and information. In actuality, these three form one entirety. If one changes, the other two will also change.

- **Hunhua happens between things in nature** — for example, the energy among trees merges and transforms between the trees. Trees of the same kind merge and transform with one another. Trees of different kinds also merge and transform with one another.

- **Hunhua happens between human beings and nature** — human qi influences plants and animals. We see this in plants and pets having different life states in different family homes. Humans can also consciously send qi to plants and animals to hunhua for vitality and healing.

- **Hunhua happens between human beings** — a group of people transform with each other.

THE ROLE OF CONSCIOUSNESS IN HUNHUA

Mingjue hunhua is different than other kinds of natural hunhua because **Mingjue hunhua is a conscious hunhua process.** The information of universal love is used to enhance the quality of life for humanity and the world.

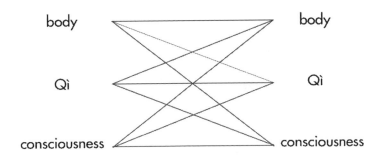

Consciousness Hunhua is the Essential Hunhua of Human Beings

Our consciousness states and the information within our consciousnesses merge and transform together. Likewise, the education received in school is a kind of consciousness hunhua.

Consciousness Merges with Consciousness

Communication is consciousness hunhua. The information in the consciousness of others comes to us, and in turn, we also send information to others. This information is also transmitted heart to heart.

Example: when a teacher instructs a student, or someone reads a book (the book expresses the information of the writer)

Consciousness Hunhua is the Highest Level of Hunhua

When you practice qigong, even if you do not say anything — if you simply sit there and connect your consciousness with the world consciousness field — you will hunhua with the collective field. This is **Mingjue hunhua.**

Once you understand these laws of the universe and life, you can readily adopt a new program in your consciousness.

Two Related Intentions: Observing and Transforming

Observing and transforming work closely together.

Observation — the intention to observe inside the body to a deeper, finer level is a way of purifying your consciousness and qi. This is also a process of seeing the world in a deeper way — to the level of its essence.

When you observe deep inside, you are observing without judgment. Observing means that consciousness is simply reflecting what is within.

Transformation — why practice deep observation? To transform your body, qi, and consciousness to a high level. Simultaneously and naturally, when you observe something, transformation happens, even if are not thinking about transformation.

Remember the principles of Hunhua Theory: transformation is always happening as a law of the universe. So even when there is no transformation at the level of consciousness, life still follows the transformation of nature. As with the trees and rivers, there is a natural process of change.

Gongfu: a Conscious Process of Transformation

An important aspect of transformation is the intention and focus on transformation. When someone practices Mingjue and qigong, there is always an intention:

What kind of life do I want?

This information guides your energy, gives direction to your observations, and thereby transforms your consciousness and body in that way.

For example, when you simply observe your body as qi, your consciousness state (and hence, your body) is already transforming. While you may not yet have the information of what kind of state you're transforming into — because you have not yet explicitly formed an intention — this information is important; it helps direct your qi body into what you want (health, peace, vitality).

In qigong, there is a saying: "What you want, you will get!"

If you want a healthy and strong qi state, then keep this information. If it is natural beauty you want, or weight loss or wisdom, then keep these intentions.

Just remember to hold your intentions focused, *but lightly.*

Sending Information as a Function of Consciousness

Conscious transformation requires information to guide the direction of its transformation. This is a very subtle point.

In some practices and at some levels, practitioners are guided to merely observe. They are guided to release their wishes and intentions, and to only have a pure and clear observation. This is a very good practice.

In Mingjue Gongfu, we recognize that Mingjue or Pure Consciousness can send information and help create what we want. This is another function of consciousness.

Consciousness receives information — learning and knowing the laws of life and the universe. With this knowledge, we can co-create a beautiful life and a beautiful world. We also evolve to a high level of consciousness.

Consciousness also sends information — practicing with a light but focused intention.

At a certain level of consciousness, sending information and receiving information become one process.

Theories and methods are just tools
to create a state of Pure Consciousness.
The Pure Consciousness state (Mingjue)
is the real teacher.

MINGJUE HEALING

Mingjue Healing is founded on Dr. Pang Ming's Hun Yuan Entirety Theory and Yiyuanti Theory. Mingjue Healing is neither positive or wishful thinking, nor denial that physical and emotional health challenges exist. It is founded on the potential of the Mingjue state — which merges the collective consciousness field with the universal qi field — to activate healing within and through us.

HEALTH, HEALING, AND DISEASE

What is Healing?

Healing simply means the process of becoming aligned with the universe's laws of health.

Disease, on the other hand, happens when we have been attuned to, knowingly or unknowingly, the laws of disease, often for a long time.

In this living universe, our lives are always merging and transforming with all different kinds of information and energy. In this process, some laws and transformations can enhance vitality. Others can diminish it.

A Problem-Focused Consciousness

Different cultures have created many different ways of healing. Most of these paths or methods, however, are relative. It may seem that, when we focus on addressing the problem, some illnesses improve or disappear. In fact, focusing on the problem or illness can create strong attachments, which can multiply the potential of the diseased state.

The more we research an illness, the more problems we may find, and the more doctors, specialists, and hospitals we may need. For qigong, too, we can find ourselves in the same conundrum. No matter the method or path, whenever we become attached to the information of illness, we risk planting that information into the time-space structure, like little seeds.

For some, body scanning for symptoms and problems is a common habit, for either a current or past health condition. For others, the fixation is on becoming healthier, more fit. For others, even if healthy, they frequently think about going to the doctor, having health screenings with doubt and worry looming in the background. For others, if a problem is detected, the doctor or healer often has a name or diagnosis for it. The diagnosis defines the problem in the reference framework and the patient confirms it in his mind, imprinting the problem in his consciousness, which can generate more worry, fear, and qi blockages in the body.

Healing, then, becomes more difficult, because the fixation itself is an obstacle.

This is a **problem-focused consciousness.** This state makes it very difficult to resolve and fully heal the illness state. Even if a particular problem is healed, the problem-focused consciousness can easily create others. It is always **focused on struggling with and trying to solve problems.**

What Consumes and Blocks Qi to Cause Disease?

1. Emotions

2. External factors — stress, environmental factors (like food, pollution, microorganisms), relationships, worldly events

3. Genetic factors can also consume or block qi

All three of these factors can create imbalances in the body and its energy. When your consciousness receives this information, it may result in an imbalance in your consciousness, thereby creating more imbalances in the body.

For example, imagine that you get a cold. You cough. Maybe you have a fever. This information merges with your consciousness. If your consciousness is stable enough, you do not mind this very much; it is "no big deal." But if you begin to think, "This cold is awful, I hate this, I wonder what's going on, why did I get sick?" this illness risks becoming imprinted in your consciousness, aggravating the problem. The body's natural healing potential runs into blockages.

With repetitive and chronic stress, the healing potential and functions can similarly diminish, which can contribute to chronic health conditions.

> Pain and suffering come to
> everyone at different times.
> They reveal to us
> the laws of life and consciousness.

Healing: Receiving Good Information

As a method, Mingjue Healing does not focus on or attach to health problems. It focuses on the healthy state, on healthy information. Healing is more important than diagnosing the problem and focusing on the whys.

The paradox: the more someone researches a health problem, the greater the risk for attachment and fear. So first, it is important to enter a good Mingjue state and reflect, "This is not a big problem." In that neutral and balanced state, research can be done with less risk of attachment.

If you are receiving a diagnosis (or if you are a healthcare provider and you are giving someone a diagnosis), you would do well to simultaneously send good healing information — like the mantra "Hun Yuan Ling Tong" or "Haola." This allows you or your patient to go beyond the emotions or potential traumas related to the condition, into the Mingjue Entirety state, and receive the information as neutral.

Take-Home: The purpose of Mingjue Healing isn't healing, per se. It is a way to create a healthy and good life with beauty.

Illnesses as Qi

At the level of essence, all illnesses are qi. And this diseased qi space can open into and merge with the infinite universal entirety, which is so strong, harmonious, and unimaginably vast that any small part in the entirety — like an illness — can be transformed by this powerful entirety. Like a drop being absorbed by the ocean.

The Laws of Healing

To change the approach, the Mingjue Gongfu student must attune to the laws of high-level health and vitality. This level goes beyond the problems to the essence of healing. So the problems can naturally change and eventually disappear.

The information of "Haola!" ("All is well!") can penetrate deeply into our hearts, minds, and bodies.

In Mingjue Healing, a high-level method of healing, we orient ourselves to the Source of life — the Original Hun Yuan Qi — to reclaim our original power, which is already within our consciousness. It is up to each individual to trust this original power, which brings us and others to the original perfect state.

When consciousness is in a pure, harmonious state, the body naturally becomes healthier and happier, too. In deep Mingjue state, if you have a strong trust in your healing potential and feel how your qi body is harmonious and healthy and how it readily flows in exchange with universal qi, this is the practice of the healthy entirety state.

This is the law of healing in action.

According to Zhineng Qigong and Mingjue Entirety Theory, the laws or conditions of complete health include:

- Attunement to the awakening Mingjue entirety

- A consciousness that is free, wise and flexible, manifesting at the levels of Mingjue and Yiyuanti (True Self)

- Relationships that are harmonious, centered, peaceful, and confident — based on universal love

- A body in which qi flows well, and bodily qi merges and transforms with external qi in good balance

- Life functions that work well — healthy, strong, and complete (manifesting on the levels of consciousness and qi)

- A body that is strong, flexible, and beautiful

When you live according to the laws, factors, and conditions of health, your life will be healthy. You do not need to focus on the problems in order to heal them. Rather, simply abide by the laws of health to enhance your life.

Going Beyond, Seeing Through, and Creating a New Life

Mingjue goes beyond the material (physical) world. So Mingjue responds to any and all situations with, "No problem!" This "no problem" consciousness state lies at the root of healing all mental, emotional, and physical problems.

Mingjue observation allows us to observe deep within ourselves in a peaceful and centered way, opening us up to see through all our blockages. Put another way, we observe our blockages and problems, but we do not mind them.

The human body is not fixed or hard. It changes every second. A person today is different than tomorrow. By always holding this in mind, the Mingjue Gongfu student can always experience renewal.

With health challenges, too, the body is always changing. This is a natural law of the universe. If the mind becomes fixated on the condition, you may consciously or unconsciously limit the possibilities for change. Aim to consciously hold in your awareness the natural law of change.

The Steps in Mingjue Healing

1. First, accept your health challenges — come to the "no problem" state in pure Mingjue and remain in this state. Observe the problem, but do not fixate on it. Keep your consciousness centered, stable, and peaceful. It is as if you are **aware of your problem as an objective observer**, seeing it from a third-person vantage point. It is not a strong attachment in your consciousness.

2. See through the reference framework — know that attachments and fixations are the root of the problem, and this includes physical, emotional and mental illnesses. Because we are conditioned to attaching to our bodies and our bodies undergo many changes, it is easy to jump to thinking there is a problem. So loosen your attachments. Attach to nothing! Then your consciousness becomes free and healthy. This high-level consciousness can transform the qi body and manage it well.

3. Use positive information to transform the qi body — there are several ways, included in great detail in the Practices and Methods section that follows.

• Mingjue Healing, or ñ Healing — ñ itself is healing information. So whenever someone says ñ in the Mingjue state, healing is happening. Trust this.

• Mingjue state is itself a healing state — it is "healing but not healing," because there is no intention of healing. It just happens because this state resonates with the laws of health. When you understand and trust that practicing the Mingjue state is a kind of healing, its potential to heal becomes more powerful.

• "Haola!" ("All is well!") — this is the information of Mingjue love, happiness, and health combined together into a single powerful healing mantra.

Hao La

Levels of Healing

Life is an entirety state of consciousness that includes internal and external qi, as well as the physical body. The following levels or dimensions of healing are actually just one entirety, but for the purpose of learning, they can be broken down into different levels.

1. At the physical level — the body becomes stronger, more flexible, and more beautiful.

2. At the qi level — health means that the qi of the body is flowing well, and that the body's qi merges and transforms with the external qi (the qi of the natural world and the universe beyond) in a good balance.

To enhance the flow of bodily qi, we can practice qi, and practice Level One (Lift Qi Up Pour Qi Down) and Level Two (Body Mind Method). But practicing the methods alone is not enough because, if emotions are present while practicing Levels One and Two, they may block the flow of qi. Or if someone's consciousness is not stable, focused, pure, and relaxed — or if it is not merged with the collective Mingjue consciousness field — the ideas and thoughts of the ego mind (reference framework) can also block qi.

Optimally, practicing qi is based on the pure Mingjue state. In this state, consciousness doesn't create any attachments or blockages, and qi can freely flow during different dynamic methods.

3. At the level of Mingjue — the practice does not need to include a lot of methods. "Good practice" means to remain in the awakened Mingjue entirety state.

If you can maintain the Mingjue state for a minute, your life can move in the direction of health. If you can remain there for an hour or a day, this harmonious entirety state will continuously improve, increasing in stability. This is a high-level healing.

It is not necessary to think about healing the problem areas, because the transformation naturally happens.

The awakening harmonious entirety state is the healthy state.

4. At the level of Yiyuanti — this is the Dao Heart in daily life. At this level, nothing serves as a blockage or triggering event. There is nothing to attach to. It is a state of true and total confidence. You have universal love. You *are* universal love.

Dao Heart

5. At the level of the "super healthy" state — your life functions have improved, moving from unhealthy or dysfunctional states to healthy ones. You are also going beyond the general idea of what health is. That is, you continue to train toward a super healthy state. This means, through practicing consciousness and qi and the body, that the functions of **consciousness, qi, and body all come to the "super ability state."** Consciousness becomes more powerful than ordinary consciousness, transcending the five sensory perceptions. The body's functions also develop super abilities. For example, someone might easily carry 200 kg! The Mingjue practitioner arrives at **the complete human state**: at the True Self and the life entirety of the True Self.

> We must always hold
> this question in mind:
> What entirety state is
> the foundation of health?

(Answer: pure Mingjue love, peace, happiness, gratitude. Trust is also paramount. If you feel this basic health entirety state is not strong enough when you are practicing Mingjue Healing, this indicates that you have room to grow in your trust of yourself and the collective field.)

MINGJUE HEALING TO IMPROVE GONGFU

In addition to benefiting others, Mingjue Healing is an effective and powerful method to practice and improve Mingjue. In fact, the purpose of healing is to practice Mingjue Gongfu: the observer comes to observe itself more clearly. Who is sending the healing information? Mingjue.

When applying Mingjue Healing to others, it is paramount to stay in a stable Mingjue state, merged with the collective consciousness field and qi universe, and remain unattached to the person who needs healing — even if this person is yourself — and also unattached to the results. How do you do this? Just focus on the observer.

Healing, then, happens as a natural side-effect.

A seeming paradox: by doing Mingjue Healing to improve Mingjue and not focusing on the outcome, the healing becomes more powerful.

Attachments to the healing effects can easily create attachments. We can more easily forget Mingjue, lose ourselves, and block the healing potential.

How to Hold Intention for Healing

There is a subtle but clear intention that Mingjue always holds: **an intention to merge.**

Mingjue Healing can be done two ways:

1. **"Healing but not healing," or simply practicing Mingjue** — the practitioner comes to the Mingjue state, continues to practice Mingjue, and doesn't mind the body. At this level, there is no separation between the one receiving and the one sending the healing, so there is no idea of "healing." With this practice, health and balance and beauty are restored but it is because it is the true Mingjue state.

2. **Mingjue practices inside the body** — Mingjue practices itself in the space you want to heal — in yourself or someone else. This brings a deeper intention to connect to and transform that space. Once you focus into that place, it is a higher practice to not think about it anymore. Just practice Mingjue within that space. This gentle healing intention can transform the body more effectively.

Super abilities information is also very powerful. Everyone has super abilities hidden within — this is an upgraded version of healing (see the subsequent section on Super Abilities).

> The most important matter
> in healing is knowing
> who we are (the observer).

Two Kinds of Healing Power

1. Natural healing power — the body contains within its DNA code the information for healing, and can heal itself regardless of whether our minds are thinking of healing or not. Often, when we have symptoms, our mind fixates on the symptoms. This worry, fear, impatience, or expectation can block the full potential of innate healing.

2. Conscious informational healing power — in some situations, even if the mind is in a free state, the body may not heal the underlying imbalances on its own. We can train our minds to be coherent, calm, and open. Mingjue can say, "No problem! The body can heal," and can send good information to the body (Haola!) and support the body's natural healing power.

HIGH-LEVEL CONSCIOUSNESS IN HEALING

Healing the entirety. Mingjue Healing is different from healing a specific problem. Rather, it heals the entirety — that is, the internal and the external conditions together. This healing happens in the reference framework: thoughts, emotions, logical thinking, worldviews, the physical body, and relationships. It is a transformation of the entirety.

Unconditional (universal) love. When consciousness returns to itself from the attachments of the external world, merges completely with the qi body, and goes deeper and deeper, this is a way to practice loving ourselves unconditionally. The act of loving ourselves from this state of Pure Consciousness can heal all trauma, pain, and suffering, and give us a completely new and beautiful life.

The inner healer. Everyone has this great and natural power within — a life power, the inner healer. By remaining in this state, the natural functions of life are restored into balance. As the natural healing power occurs again and again, the renewal we experience continues again, too.

Once you learn to use a free consciousness state to send good information and love the body, the quality of the body will improve. Then you can realize that the transformation of the physical body is not only a natural process decided by your DNA code. Rather, the state of the body is a conscious life process decided by your consciousness.

Conscious healing. High-level consciousness can change the natural processes of life (conscious hunhua as opposed to natural hunhua). Over a person's lifetime, some natural information will influence his life and health. More importantly, his consciousness state can either create blockages in this natural process or remain open to flow, greatly affecting his overall health.

Longevity. High-level consciousness also works on extending the natural lifespan — longevity. A high-level consciousness state draws in more qi to nourish and transform the body, harmonizing within. A harmonized body can extend its life beyond what we may think is possible for the natural human lifespan.

Healing Story: a Woman with Multiple Tumors

A woman with multiple tumors went to Teacher Wei for healing. She laid herself on a bed and, having received his healing information, she suddenly felt an enormous change. She went to the toilet several times. Instead of feeling tired, she felt more vigorous. Two days later, she visited the hospital to have her reproductive system checked. To the doctor's surprise, a big tumor had disappeared and a few smaller tumors had shrunken to half their original size.

When Teacher Wei was doing the healing, he simply stayed in a deep Mingjue (pure, universal consciousness) state and sent her good information. In the Mingjue state, he merged with her qi body. Her qi body was in his Mingjue consciousness field. Then he gently sent this information: "The inner qi is open and flowing well, all the blockages have already disappeared." It was very simple.

Relationships Between Mind and Body

- **The Mind as the Slave of the Body** — in Mingjue Gongfu practice, "body" means the physical body and its sensory organs. Usually, consciousness fixates on and attaches to the sensory organs and its physical sensations. In this state, consciousness is not autonomous. It is the slave of the physical body and reacts to whatever happens inside.

- **Mingjue as the Master** — if consciousness remains in Mingjue state, then Mingjue becomes the independent observer. In this independent state, Mingjue is itself, so Mingjue can freely send and receive information, and can guide the body. Mingjue uses the physical sensations as neutral information. In other words, Mingjue has learned to use the sensory organs as a tool through which to experience life.

MINGJUE EMOTIONAL HEALING

What Are Emotions?

An emotion is the total sum reaction that happens at the following three levels (all three levels are affected):

- The body (sensations)
- Qi (energy change)
- Consciousness (a trigger of information)

If a strong emotion like anger or fear arises, some kind of information has triggered your consciousness and its state. Sometimes the information is received by the sensory organs; you see, feel, hear, or touch something that your consciousness doesn't like. Then the body's energy changes quickly, and strong feelings ensue.

Mingjue Emotional Healing teaches us how to move from the reflex or instinct level to the conscious wisdom state and freedom.

Mingjue and Trauma

Many people can remember childhood traumas, more recent ones, or other difficult experiences. The Mingjue-level practice does not focus a lot on clearing specific blockages in consciousness — there is no need to analyze or judge them or to even know what they are. The practice simply focuses on purifying and stabilizing Mingjue itself.

By not focusing on the past, the focus remains on pure Mingjue, which is always in the present moment. A new way of thinking and relating happens, a new pattern for the reference framework. In pure Mingjue, you can receive good information, universal love, compassion, inner peace, happiness, and beauty.

When lived from this state, a new life can emerge and develop, step by step. Why focus on cleaning up the past when you can readily enter the present and go beyond it?

This is a very simple, direct way to a new life.

EMOTIONS AND SENSATIONS IN THE REFERENCE FRAMEWORK

Emotions and bodily sensations are important aspects of experiencing life. Some emotions and sensations are more challenging, others more comfortable. All of these experiences contribute to a complete and beautiful life.

When an experience or thought acts as a trigger, it is triggering the reference framework. The important thing is to observe the emotions and sensations and thoughts, and not get attached to them. That doesn't mean that they aren't "real." In fact, by not being attached, emotions and sensations can be experienced in more fullness and freedom.

Most problems and conflicts arise from people not knowing how to manage and go beyond their emotions. Fear and self-protectiveness separate us from the entirety state. Fear and worry also consume a lot of qi and diminish overall health and vitality.

Two Kinds of Happiness

Most if not all people want to find happiness. There are two general kinds:

1. One kind of happiness comes from external events and circumstances (like singing, dancing, etc.) that make us happy. This is an external, conditional kind of happiness.

2. Another kind of happiness comes from the inner depths of consciousness — from the integration of consciousness merging with the internal qi of the body. When observation is practiced deeply enough, the experience of happiness will naturally emerge. Mind and heart are totally open as you go beyond all kinds of attachments and fixations. Mingjue Gongfu practices this kind of state.

Mingjue Manages Life and Emotions

Mingjue Gongfu is a practice for life. This means that when we practice the methods, we are practicing; and when we are living our daily lives, we are also practicing.

If you find yourself practicing Mingjue Gongfu for 60 minutes a day, then going about the rest of your day in the ordinary consciousness, the quality of your consciousness has not yet changed. You are still focused on external people, events, and things. This includes your work and ideas, too.

Attachments can make life feel beautiful, funny, and abundant! But they can also make life feel difficult because they can create a lot of emotional blockages — so attachments are not the same as true abundance.

Two Levels of Yiyuanti that Cause Fixed Emotions

1. **Self Yiyuanti reference framework (infancy)** — a sense that there is a "self" and this sense of self stays in our consciousness and becomes fixed there. This is the foundation of emotions. Usually this happens at the instinctual level. Our bodies want to feel good and want to survive. This begins at the time of

infancy. This sense of self becomes incorporated into the pure Yiyuanti.

2. **Distorted Yiyuanti reference framework (adulthood)** — the sense of a separate self develops into a fixed framework in adulthood. Right and wrong, mine and yours. This ego is the foundation of emotions. Once we have emotional experiences, we remember these emotions and create conditioned responses.

Emotions and Information

For most people, emotions are just a fixed system of information. This means that the reference framework receives information, and this information triggers qi changes in the body, then emotions develop in Yiyuanti. New information triggers the reference framework and makes more emotional reactions. This is how emotional memory develops.

Emotions and Yiyuanti

- Emotions are not made by external information. They are reactions that result from Yiyuanti (or Mingjue) losing itself. When we don't lose ourselves, Yiyuanti just receives the information in a neutral state.

- When Yiyuanti loses itself, emotions limit the function of Yiyuanti and diminish the purity of the qi of Yiyuanti — consciousness cannot reflect things with the clarity of a mirror. Minds become fuzzy and confused ("a mess"), and the mirror is masked by smudges.

- **High-level state** — when Yiyuanti is awakened, it can play with emotions to mobilize qi. That is, emotions are a tool that Yiyuanti (or Mingjue) can use to benefit self and others. Mingjue Gongfu practices at this level. Similarly, Mingjue can use bodily sensations to feel energy, all in the free state.

If Mingjue chooses anger: Mingjue can observe the anger at the same time you experience the anger, then use the anger to mobilize the qi of the liver without hurting yourself (in Qigong Theory, the organ associated with anger is the liver).

If Mingjue chooses happiness: You can be happy, but you will not lose yourself in the happiness either.

> Emotions are not made by external information.
> They result from Yiyuanti (or Mingjue) losing itself.

Practice: You can do dress rehearsals and play with different emotions.

You enter into a good Mingjue state, then elicit fear, anger, sadness, or worry. Practice observing these experiences as an independent observer. This can not only help develop Mingjue in the moment, it can help Mingjue be more stable when life events trigger the same emotions.

Consciousness Guides the Right Use of Energy

Food, money, cars, houses, our bodies — they are all energy.

Some energy is natural, other forms are created by man's consciousness (Example: houses, cars, and money).

Mingjue manages information, information manages energy, and energy manages the whole world.

Mingjue is also qi — it's a high-level, conscious energy. High-level energy manages lower-level energy. This is a law of life.

At the body level, emotions directly influence the immune system. With different emotions, the inner organs will produce different hormones, and these hormones influence the immune system.

The Effects of Emotions

- **Physical changes** — chemistry and biological changes happen in response to emotions. Because emotions change energy and energy fields, they also affect people around us.

- **Energy level** — different emotions influence the qi of the Five Organ System in Qigong Theory. Strong emotions influence our rational thinking and thoughts. Strong emotions can also influence the thinking of others around us. Regret often follows rash or poor decisions that were controlled by strong emotions.

- **Consciousness level** — Yiyuanti, thoughts, wisdom. Emotions can act like dust or smudges on the mirror of Yiyuanti and distort its clarity. Emotions can distort or block the wisdom we receive and also our thoughts. Strong, fixed emotions are like pollution for the collective consciousness field — and when lots of people have strong emotions, they affect the field exponentially. Qigong teachers must always cultivate a peaceful Mingjue state before teaching or guiding, leading from their best states. More so, this state can be cultivated throughout our daily lives and all our relationships.

- **Collective consciousness field** — you influence others and others influence you. If you experience strong emotions that diminish your power or concentration to connect to the field, you can focus on developing trust — trust that the field will provide that power and support you. Anyone who practices Mingjue methods contributes positively to the field.

RIGHT ATTITUDE ON EMOTIONS

Accept your emotions. Don't resist or begrudge them; that will only fuel them.

Use your emotions to adjust your qi and life. Emotions can serve to activate energy and empower change in your life. For example, let's say your heart is closed, there is no power, no love. Then something triggers anger in you. If you learn to harness this activated energy behind the emotion, it can serve to open your heart and give you courage. So we can learn to harness the energy behind emotions.

Cultivate positive emotions. Positive emotions are healing. Happy emotions can break through all other emotions.

Master your emotions. Know how to harness your emotions instead of being enslaved by them. This is what Mingjue Gongfu teaches. You learn that you are not your emotions, and instead, learn to observe them.

Go beyond the fixed emotional state. According to Daode Theory, Daode values are harmony, happiness, natural state, and dignity. Your consciousness state is not dictated by your emotions, but is in accordance with the higher-level Daode values.

Resolving Negative Emotions in the Moment

1. Come to the observer — Mingjue appears. If Yiyuanti is clear and stable enough, triggering events cannot influence it, and emotions will disappear. This is the most direct and high-level practice.

2. Observe the causes of the emotions — see that they have passed. There is no cause now. Only emptiness.

3. Observe the emotions — notice that they are empty, they are qi.

4. Understand what emotions are — they are reactions of the fixed reference framework, which forces the self to fixate on the past or worry about the future.

5. Transform the emotions — change any challenging emotions with positive emotions or information. At the Huaxia Center, before practice or teaching, Dr. Pang would always encourage the "happy quarter," or the 15 minutes before the session, to share humorous stories, laugh together, make angry or anxious faces and turn them into happy ones. "I am love! I am compassion!"

6. Release the emotions — Zhineng Qigong usually does not focus on this method, because its focus is on *transforming* emotions. But if it is difficult to transform emotions in the heated moment, releasing them can be useful. For example: a healthy cry. **Releasing emotions cannot heal emotions, but they can release the blockages created by the emotions.** In other words, releasing emotions cannot harmonize the fixed information that caused the emotions (upstream), but can release any blockages caused by the emotions (downstream).

Four Practices to Go Beyond Emotions

1. Remain in Mingjue state and observe… observe… eventually, the emotions will dissipate.*

2. Immediately come to the observer — a state of total non-attachment.**

3. In the Mingjue Entirety state, recite the Mingjue Love Mantra: *I am Mingjue love, I am peace, I am happiness, I am gratitude.* Repeat this again and again, until it goes deep into your subconscious. You then fully *become* these states.

4. Happy gong, laughter gong, inner smile gong — a "gong" is a challenge, usually of a specified duration. Think of the Happy Buddha. Watch funny videos. Choose unconditional happiness instead of conditional happiness, the latter of which is dependent on life circumstances. Laughter and an inner smile can harness the energy of emotions to heal the qi of internal organs and also transform negative emotions.

> True healing information
> comes from the heart (state of being),
> more than the mouth or hands.

SEEING THROUGH TRAUMA

Much of the healing of emotions happens at the level of *energy.* Trauma, however, lies deeper and subtler — **at the level of *information.*** To heal and transform emotional trauma, Mingjue Gongfu students learn to see through the trauma and understand it.

---

* These practice are explained in detail in the subsequent section, Part 2: Practices and Methods.

** Idem.

A brief review of the Three Levels of Matter Theory:

1. Physical or material dimension

2. Qi or energy dimension

3. Information or consciousness dimension — this is akin to upgrading the internal operating system or programming. It is the highest level of existence and it contains the other dimensions within it.

Where Does Trauma Come From?

If Mingjue loses itself, strong information from various situations can trigger the reference framework and create fear or pain, becoming a fixed, imprinted memory. The triggering situation might include:

- Sensations from the body (Example: pain, tension)

- Sensations from the external world (Example: direct violence, extreme environmental conditions)

- Parental and family information (Example: arguing parents, abusive family)

- Collective (cultural) information — collective suffering can cause fixations in individual consciousnesses. Although this may enter consciousness in a subconscious way, it still affects the consciousness state.

- Ancestral information — difficult information from grandparents and ancestors can be passed down in the fixed time-space structure; their blocked energies can get entangled with our energies.

By learning to observe and see through this trauma as simple information, anyone can transform it. To heal ancestral trauma, the details of what happened are not important or necessary. It is simply about sending our ancestors and ourselves universal love from the Mingjue state.

Within Mingjue, all life experiences can become wisdom. The information can also become a kind of connected power, meaning that someone who faces a lot of challenges in his life can develop a stronger and stabler consciousness because all of the experiences and their information connect together to form an "information connected power." And this can, in turn, further strengthen the willpower of Mingjue.

How to Heal Trauma or Resolve Negative Emotions

Emotional trauma stays imprinted in our memories. So how do we go into and then beyond this?

1. Use the master key! — this is the first and foremost method. Always practice Mingjue and staying in Mingjue. Eventually, you will realize you are not the memories, the emotions, the pain, or the physical sensations. You are Mingjue love, peace, happiness, and gratitude. There is no need to specifically address the trauma, which is in the reference framework. You have gone beyond this dualistic framework.

2. Resolve emotional blockages peacefully — accept them, don't fight them. Observe yourself as a young child and face an early childhood trauma. First, set a good Mingjue state and trust that the Mingjue consciousness field will support you. This is very important! As you observe the traumatic event with acceptance, the most important information will appear in your memory. Usually, the strongest information has more energy and has been repeated many times. Trust that those experiences cannot control you now; they are qi and they are within the Mingjue field, too. Over time, the traumatic triggers will be reconditioned to be in the Mingjue peaceful state instead of the strong emotions.

When practicing Mingjue Healing methods, it's important to engage the process of deep observation. If you're watching or thinking of a difficult situation, do not drop into the suffering or into the emotional feeling. Just relax and observe. If any emotions or sensations emerge, still just relax and observe — as if you're observing something that is very ordinary, like a movie, or like watching the blue sky.

Observe the events as though they're just information.

> Creating a new reference framework
> is a conscious practice.

3. Change the reference framework — harmonize and open the old, fixed information that caused the trauma. Make space for a new attitude and perspective.

4. Work at the energy level — open the energy blockages created by the emotions. Transform them into good feelings. From an energy level, you can support the changing of information and consciousness.

In the reference framework, you're aiming to harmonize specific information. So it's important to try to remember the details of the traumas as much as possible and to face the experiences. Once you connect with the old, fixed information, you can consciously connect with new information.

If you cannot access a lot of details in the memories, then it is important to go beyond the reference framework into Mingjue state. In the Mingjue state, you accept everything *and* you continue to organize and harmonize the field.

Note: If you work on transforming qi blockages (at the level of energy) *simultaneously with practicing at the Mingjue consciousness level*, then the transformation can be more effective. If you just work on the information level, the process may take a little more time because the qi is blocked, too.

"Going Beyond" is Not Bypassing

"Going through and going beyond" does not mean we avoid our challenges, past or present. "Going beyond" means we can accept and face everything, that our heart remains open to life's experiences without attachments or fixations.

We do not attach to "good" events or experiences. We do not become blocked by difficult ones.

"Going beyond" means we review everything. We can easily hold everything and merge with everything in a harmonious state. Everything enters our consciousness in a free-flowing manner.

Resolving Depression

(See the subsequent section, Part 2: Methods and Practices, for more details)

1. Use simple ways to activate energy — use sounds, increasing your dynamic movements and applying more effort.

2. Receive and create positive information, consciously and actively. Choose information to make happiness.

3. Build an orderly pattern of everyday life, which can create more ordered thinking and more coherent, flowing energy.

4. See through the roots of depression.

5. Harmonize old information blockages. Accept and love them.

6. Join more social service activities in positive communities.

7. Practice Mingjue Gongfu. Go beyond your reference framework. Become your own master.

On Anxiety and Panic

Q: What would you recommend as the best response or practice for panic and anxiety that seem to be worsening?

A: It is important to change your mindset. The increasing symptoms reflect deeper imbalances coming to the surface. So you can say, "Ah, I'm glad this deeper stuff is getting triggered and coming out! Then I can accept it and it will change. No problem."

- Continually practice Mingjue Universal Love Entirety.

- Change the information you receive — go outside, walk in nature. Avoid just sitting there and thinking.

- Receive more information from nature to transform the fixed pattern of fear.

One Important Way to Bring Order into Our Lives

Answer: Silence.

Silence doesn't mean not speaking; it means quieting the mind. Silencing thoughts might initially be difficult. To make this easier, start by seeing where you might simplify your life, then make those changes.

If silence feels uncomfortable, you might find someone who will commit to this together with you.

Silence can help consciousness organize the information it receives from the external world and harmonize it, instead of creating confusion, noise, and disorganization.

In a more ordered state:

- Learning becomes more efficient; the reference framework is organized.

- Wisdom flows more readily from your heart.

- Your energy becomes organized.

- The information in your body (the DNA) can also become more organized. Example: Disorganized energy in the liver expresses as anger. When it is organized, it expresses as courage.

BUILDING A HEALTHY STATE (YOU ALREADY KNOW HOW)

1. Practice qi to nourish the body and Yiyuanti — before Mingjue is stable and strong enough, reduce as many external triggers as possible. This can give you space to improve the purity and steadiness of Mingjue. With fewer triggers, Mingjue can easily merge with the qi emptiness. Practice silent meditation. Stay connected to Mingjue Love. When your Mingjue matures and becomes stronger, you can face stronger triggers without problem.

2. [Outer engagement] Choose to receive more hopeful, beautiful, and happy information — as stated above, when Mingjue is stable and strong enough, negative information will not affect you in the same way. Nonetheless, as you heal and further develop Mingjue, it is important to consciously choose higher-level communities and information.

Sometimes you will encounter groups of people who have a lot of drama and disordered energy. If you cannot serve the group by co-cultivating more coherence, it may be wise not continue with them and to join other groups where there is healthier information and more free-flowing energy.

3. [Internal engagement] Cultivate more ordered, positive thinking — create happiness in your everyday life and observe the value of your life. This helps your consciousness to become healthier.

Engage in activities that bring you joy.

Serve others in the community.

Bring order to your life — external order reflects a more harmonized internal reference framework.

4. Cultivate will power and discipline to change old habits and conditioned thinking — reduce the influence of negative information and support positive information.

5. The master key: practice Mingjue — go beyond all the fixations.

Conscious Decision Theory

We have free will to choose our internal states. Consciousness can directly decide and determine our life state. This free will uses life itself as its manifestation.

I want to be happy. *Okay, I am happy.*

I want to be peaceful. *Okay, I am peaceful.*

Are you happy? *Yes, I am happy.*

The Story of Two Wolves

There is a famous story from the Native American tradition about a wise grandfather teaching his grandson about two wolves. One is good, the other is bad. The grandson asked the grandfather, "If they fight, which wolf will win?" The grandfather replied, "The one you feed."

Everybody's heart contains two wolves — one positive, the other negative. If we always feed the positive wolf, it will win. That is why it is important that Mingjue feels, receives, sends, and creates beautiful and healthy information.

Important: At the same time, we need to go *beyond* the duality of the two wolves. At the Mingjue level, both wolves are accepted and loved unconditionally. Mingjue observes them both in the entirety. This is the true way to go beyond the notion of separateness and respond to morality in a free state instead of a fixed one.

Story from China: Healing as a Scientific Experiment

Some years ago in China, a group of qigong teachers did an elaborate experiment to test qigong science and gongfu abilities. One by one, different teachers went into a Pure Consciousness state and sent information to a machine to generate electromagnetic energy. Usually, the effect was weak if the consciousness state was not pure or relaxed enough. It was also weak, however, if the intention was too strong.

The teachers only needed very subtle information within their consciousness, without attaching to any information — to simply sit, be still, pure, and empty, and enter the **"do nothing"** (*ru ding*) **state**. In this very pure state, the simplest information appeared, as if it was no information. The teachers trusted without a doubt that the magnetic energy was already happening; as if they saw the magnetism reflected in their Pure Consciousness. In these moments, the results were usually positive. That is, the machine readings really changed and the results were verified.

The use of consciousness to change the quantum (the finest measurable quantity of radiant energy at the time of this writing) is also like this. So everything we ask our consciousness to manifest does manifest, as long as the focus is not on the external world of forms. This is the essential meaning of the adage, "Change yourself, change the world."

Healing others is also a scientific experiment. There is an important dimension to healing living things, which is different than changing inorganic things — and that is universal love.

In the collective Mingjue field, there is no separation or judgment. Deep universal love means loving your family members, all human beings, yourself, the natural world — you love everything unconditionally. This is a Mingjue Universal Love Healing Entirety.

> When we heal with universal love,
> it can awaken our deepest potential.

THE TRUE VALUE OF YOUR LIFE

In the universe, there is an infinite amount of information. And all the information is continually merging and transforming. Usually, we prefer to limit or resist change. Or we want to control what happens. Both are fixations; both can create pain and suffering — even if our intentions are well-meaning.

The process of merging and transforming in the entirety can create a new reality in every moment. The information in everyone's individual consciousness is just one tiny contributor of information in the entirety. So in this vast information universe, what is the value of your life?

Here are two steps toward discovering it:

1. Observe, accept, and enjoy the process of being truly alive. This can open your heart.

2. Ask yourself this essential question, "What information am I living my life by?" Your Mingjue (Pure Consciousness) reflects and joins the vast matrix of information — from society, the world, and the universe — to merge and transform with it. And although it doesn't always feel like it, you have a choice in what information you bring to the universal matrix.

When you fully realize these two steps, you become an active participant in the process of creation — a co-creator of your life and the collective field. At any time, you can choose to contribute Mingjue love, peace, happiness, and gratitude. When you continue to develop your Mingjue, the information you send into the collective field will have greater power to transform. That is, weaker information will follow yours.

This is the true value of your life.

Co-Creating with Difficult Experiences

When we are stricken with guilt or other chronic, strong emotions like anger or grief, this represents an attachment to the past. These thoughts and emotions press upon you and consume a lot of energy, suppressing your potential for courage and unconditional love.

Applying the two steps above, you can:

1. Accept your guilt as a habit of the past and a habit of the ego mind. Come to the present moment and accept it. If this is difficult, try connecting to any bodily sensations you may feel when you think about your guilt. Observe these sensations as qi that is always flowing. Do not resist them. Just let them flow. Soon they will disappear. **This is merging and transforming as a natural process.**

2. Activate your insight and connect to "good information." See that the experience of guilt is guiding you to see your internal state: "Oh, there is a fixed judgment there. The judgment is an old, conditioned pattern." Who is observing this? Mingjue observes and illuminates all. Mingjue also says "Haola! No problem!" and does not fixate on the outcome. If the guilt disappears, that is wonderful. If not, embrace the present reality with an equally open heart. By making the subconscious conscious, the old patterns are no longer the master. **This is merging and transforming as a conscious process.**

In this manner, Mingjue continues to choose good information to contribute to the collective field.

MINGJUE RELATIONSHIPS AND LOVE

The phrase "Mingjue Relationships" means that we connect with everything and everyone as one. That is, we first come to and remain in a Mingjue state — a universal love state, a state of oneness. Then this awakening love flows through us and affects all the different relationships in our lives. When this is the internal foundation, all relationships become harmonious. Mingjue Relationships are awakened in and by universal love.

> *I am you.*
> > *You are me.*
> > > *We are one.*
> > > > *I love you.*
> > > > *You love me.*
> > > *I love us.*
> > *We love me.*
> *We are love.*

"We are love" is the foundation for Mingjue Relationships among human beings.

Note: Universal love is not an emotion. It is a state of being that is peaceful, quiet, and harmonious.

A Story from Teacher Wei

"Many years ago, while I was watching a movie of Mother Theresa, I stood in Standing Meditation posture. I felt her compassion and universal love, and it touched me deeply. My inner space was very peaceful and quiet. Suddenly, I felt two warm streams of energy rise up from my abdomen to my eyes. Tears began to flow. There were no emotions associated with these tears. It was very peaceful, very comfortable. Later, I shared this experience with my friend. I asked him about it, as I had never had this kind of experience before. He explained that these were tears of compassion, that Mother Theresa's story activated inner compassion."

PRINCIPLES OF MINGJUE RELATIONSHIPS

To understand Mingjue Relationships, we must understand them from the reference framework of Mingjue or Yiyuanti Theory. This forms the foundational principles of true, loving relationships and how to interact with others and the world.

The Fundamental Relationship: Yiyuanti and Information

All relationships are manifestations of Yiyuanti and the information it contains.

Before Mingjue Gongfu, when we wanted to change our relationships, we would likely focus on the external world. For example, if we had a conflict with a partner or child, we might focus on the other person causing the problem and needing to change.

From Mingjue awareness, partners and children are one with us. Mingjue sees through these relationships, deep within, and from Mingjue we can change the information. We can rewrite the program inside of us, like a game. And we are confident we can change it.

Yiyuanti Reflects Information

Relationships form when Yiyuanti reflects information. Put another way, Mingjue receives information, and then the relationship forms. Whether the relationship is harmonious or not depends on whether we lose the Mingjue state. When we have lost ourselves to the external world, including to those with whom we are in relationship, we fixate on that information. We use our reference framework to judge. Emotions emerge.

In the Mingjue state, we do not attach to external triggers. We can receive information, remain centered, peaceful, and clear. We can even use the reference framework to judge the information in a neutral way. We do not fixate on it.

If we are stable and powerful enough, the other person(s) can be transformed, too, because our information transforms the entirety, which includes us and the other(s).

The Reference Framework and Mingjue Relationships

The foundation of Mingjue Relationships is the reference framework made by Yiyuanti receiving information.

Our reference framework participates in our relationships. In the Mingjue state, Yiyuanti (or Mingjue) uses our reference framework as a tool to create and influence relationships. When we receive information in Mingjue, that information merges and transforms (hunhua) with the information that already exists within our reference framework.

Outside of Mingjue, our reference frameworks decide the nature and expression of our relationships.

Central Information

Within our reference frameworks, there is a lot of information. But one kind of information is very strong, highlighted above the others — this is called the "central information." All the other related information follows this central information as an information system or thought chain.

The central information within our reference framework decides the state in our relationships. This is why the states of our relationships can change from one to another — because our reference framework plays different roles in different relationships, guided by whatever our central information is. This central information informs us, consciously or subconsciously, how to respond or react. Essentially, we manifest and become whatever is contained in the central information.

When we relate to others as the Mingjue inner observer, the central information changes. We learn to observe our relationships without attachments. The observer itself becomes the central information.

Mingjue as the Central Information

The Mingjue state is the most powerful information.

When the observer observes itself, the observer becomes highlighted within itself. "I am in this present moment. I am the central information." We are this peaceful state.

So while we also receive other information, we know we are just playing our role. No matter what happens or who we are in relationship with, the central information remains the same: *I am Mingjue, I am love, I am peace.* The other information is not central any more.

Central Information and Thoughts

At any given moment, there are many fragments of information competing in our Yiyuanti. But at this very moment, why does one particular piece of information emerge from our consciousness as a thought? Because the central information is guiding this process. In other words, when the quality of some information is very clear and strong, it becomes the central information.

In the Mingjue state, Mingjue is the central information. Mingjue can also reflect other fragments of information within the reference framework and remain in an awakening, clear state. Mingjue is at the center while, at the same time, reflecting all kinds of information about life and the universe.

When information other than Mingjue itself is highlighted, that information becomes what we call thoughts. We can say that this is the "secondary central information."

Note: There can be additional levels of information that emerge in Yiyuanti. But most people can only realize whatever the central information is. Mingjue practitioners may come to realize two or three levels of information by clear insight or observation.

Another situation is when the information connects together and becomes an "information chain." In this case, the information in the chain becomes more powerful than when it is not connected together. When new knowledge is acquired and there are many related topics, this forms a "knowledge system," which is more powerful than an information chain.

Single Information, Complex Information, and Information Chains

The sound practice of ñ is an example of single information.* There is no meaning, so it cannot connect to or link with other information.

The word "universe" is an example of complex information. "Universe" contains the information of everything in the universe. So this single word contains an infinite number of other fragments of information.

An information chain is a logical series of connections. When we think of something, a logical chain of reasoning connects one information to another, by association. This gathers a lot of power.

Single Information and the Power of Repetition

Usually, single information is not as powerful as an information chain.

Through repetition, however, the single information of ñ increases in power. This is the power of repeating mantras and chants over and over again, ten thousand times.

Single information is so simple that it can go through the whole reference framework — this is a special feature of ñ. Because simple information has no time-space structure or meaning, it is more flexible and can go through the whole reference framework, coming directly to Yiyuanti.

Mingjue Transforms the Entirety and Forms the New Information Order

When we choose a fragment of positive information, this information connects with related information in the reference framework and becomes more powerful. It can transform our qi and physical body states, since our qi and physical body follow the information they are given.

---

* See Part 2: Methods and Practices, for details on the practice of ñ.

Sending more powerful information also enhances our willpower. This willpower is the power of Mingjue — a direct kind of power. Mingjue chooses the information, sends the information, and trusts the information.

This is how Mingjue gradually forms a new information order of life. Mingjue chooses information and reference frameworks to make decisions in the present moment and in the entirety.

Summary: The changes in our relationships do not happen from the outside, but from within. So when we seek changes in our relationships, we need to rewrite the program from within ourselves. With the information of Mingjue and Yiyuanti, we need to reflect upon how to change our relationships.

HOW RELATIONSHIPS CAN MANIFEST

In fixed relationships, the state is fixed and conditional.

- **Dependence and independence** — sometimes we depend on different things and different people. At other times, we remain independent.

- **Attachment and detachment** — sometimes we attach to something. At other times, we detach. This is the nature and the dynamic of relationships.

- **Control and freedom** — sometimes we want to control something, and at other times, we do not control and are free.

- **Occupying and release** — sometimes we occupy or possess something, and at other times, we release the control over it.

In Mingjue-level relationships, the state is free.

Mingjue is independent, even when it is connected to or merged with everything. It also goes beyond everything. It is a centered state. Because it is independent and also merged with the collective consciousness field, Mingjue can receive and give unconditional love.

For Mingjue to be independent and stable, willpower plays a very important role.

This is the foundation of high-level relationships. When Mingjue works in our daily lives and relationships, we realize that relationships are within our consciousness.

> Mingjue changes fixed relationships
> into free relationships with
> unconditional love.

HOW TO CHANGE AND HEAL RELATIONSHIPS

Changing and healing relationships require an internal transformation of information and the reference framework. This process asks us to:

- Remain stable in a Mingjue Entirety state

- Consciously change our thoughts and our worldview

- Observe Mingjue as it repeats beautiful and positive information

- Observe Mingjue sending good information, transforming the entirety, strengthening willpower, and forming the new information order of life

With a good, stable Mingjue state, many relationships can change, even if the patterns have been closed or blocked for a long time. This is because our Mingjue Entirety state merges with the other person(s) in the family or community. And since the Mingjue Entirety state *is* universal peace and love, we *are* peace and love, too.

When We Fight with Others: We are thinking of ourselves as separate, therefore creating more blockages in ourselves and others. Instead of fighting, we can ask the following questions:

1. At the relative level —

    How can I create more harmony and peace in this situation?

    How can I lift up that person's life?

2. At the Mingjue level —

    Who is observing this siutation?

    Who am I?

When Others Fight with Us: This means they need love. They are losing themselves to the external world, stuck in their small ego identities, stuck in the fear of the loss of their material (physical) sense of life, and stuck in their reference frameworks, even well-meaning belief systems like religion and justice.

A Word of Caution: If we do not first connect to Mingjue peace and love and the collective field, our intentions become an ego state. "I want to create harmony!" And yet underneath, there is a push energy — anger, worry, and fixation have already taken hold. The righteous ego fights with the angry ego. Internal fighting and suffering ensue. These blockages occur at the information level.

Suggestions from Dr. Pang

When you have thoughts, stay in the Mingjue state and clearly observe your thoughts. If the thought is negative, if it is not good for life or for the entirety, then do not follow that thought. You have to catch it, which means to realize it with clarity, in the moment. So if the thought does not serve your life or the entirety, you catch it, and release it.

As for negative emotions, the old habit of the reference framework would have you follow these negative emotions, and to feel and express them. For example, if someone says something negative, the mind might think, "I do not like this, I hate this, I need to stick up for myself," and it is easy to fixate on the words, making it difficult to release them. When you get stuck, you convince yourself that you have a right to be angry.

Now you have another choice: to change this conditioned response and stay in the Mingjue state.

Summary

In Mingjue Relationships, we:

- Observe, check, and change.
- Judge and think less.
- Love more.

THE DEEPEST RELATIONSHIP: MINGJUE AND ITSELF

When most people think of relationships, it usually has to do with someone else, or with a group of others. The deepest and most significant relationship, however, is between Mingjue and itself.

A Relationship of Self-Reflection

In the relationship of Mingjue and itself, the reflection and the reflected are one. Mingjue reflects everything in life and in the universe as a mirror. This includes all relationships and Mingjue itself.

What happens over time, as described earlier in Yiyuanti Theory, is that as a child develops awareness through the five senses, Mingjue begins to lose awareness of itself, focusing externally instead. Relationships, then, are all externally focused, too. We feel separate from others. "I am me, you are you."

This conditioned experience of duality is the starting place of Mingjue Gongfu. New students usually think, "The observer observes itself."

But if we are already the observer, why do we observe ourselves? We only need to *be* ourselves, to *know* ourselves.

I am the observer.

I am.

So it is important to realize and directly experience the unity level of reality.

A Note on Enlightenment

Enlightenment is simply when Mingjue becomes itself, when the observer and the observed become one. There is no subject and object any more.

Many people come to know who they are for a period of time and observe the observer; but there is still a very small separation between the observer and the observed. This is not true enlightenment. This is just the *preparation* for enlightenment.

When you can observe increasingly with more purity, depth, and stability, with uninterrupted concentration and relaxation, even when external triggering events occur, this is the foundation of enlightenment. When Mingjue reflects itself, the separation begins to disappear (this is called **lingyuan** 灵元).

Then one day, when the preparation and foundation are ripe enough, some piece of information serves as a trigger, and suddenly, the last tiny separation breaks, the last tiny smudge clears from the mirror. Deep inside Mingjue, the complete entirety appears. **This is enlightenment.**

The truly enlightened Mingjue Gongfu student does not focus on or boast that he or she has reached enlightenment.

SEXUALITY AND LOVE

Zhineng Qigong is a science for general humanity and not a religion. The following is a general summary of Zhineng Qigong's teachings on sex and sexuality.

Sex is a basic dimension of human relationships. The potential benefits of sex include a stronger union and connection and improved energy flow.

Sexual energy is considered very important for life — it is called *xing* (pronounced, "shing").

Xing is important for vitality. It is also important for emotional states. When the xing is strong, hormones are more balanced, creating a more balanced emotional state. If too much xing is lost, the body's physical energy diminishes, and consciousness can also become less clear. Mingjue, therefore, can also become less clear — it can weaken. When sexuality is not balanced, many conflicts may arise in our relationships.

Mingmen Inner Palace

Ming Men Nei Qiao

The Mingmen Inner Palace (the empty space just anterior to L-2 and L-3 in the lumbar spine) stores innate or inherent qi. This innate qi moves through the central nervous system to nourish the internal organs, brain, and consciousness. As the internal organs become stronger, the body becomes younger, healthier and more beautiful. This can promote healthy longevity.

While a healthy sex life can enhance the connection between two people, too much sex can consume and deplete qi from the Mingmen Inner Palace.

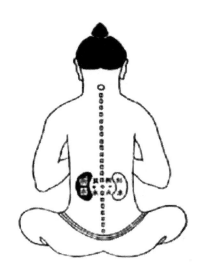

Ming Men

Affection

When deep inside the heart, the love for another person arises and an attachment forms, it can feel like we cannot live without the other person. The affection may be mutual, balanced, and affirming. In Mingjue Gongfu, however, we recognize that this can also become a fixation.

When the reference frameworks differ between people in a relationship, conflicts will most certainly arise. Mingjue accepts everything and everyone. The Mingjue state can help us understand and accept the perspectives of others, even if they are not in alignment with ours.

Note: Mingjue is a state without attachments. It is important that Mingjue does not become attached to the feelings and sensations of sexual activities.

True Love is Mingjue Love

"True love" means unconditional love. When we come to this level, we have come to the Mingjue Entirety state. Unconditional love can also be called Mingjue Love. We feel full of love on the inside, no matter what the circumstances, because we *are* love — universal love.

When this unconditional love manifests between partners, they share the same dream: both want to go to a higher level and to serve the world. They work together and support each other. Mingjue love connects them together, even if their name for it is not Mingjue. In this state, love is free. Some may call this "soulmates." There is an independence and a mutual appreciation. At the same time, they also support each other to improve their consciousness. Even if, at times, the relative connection isn't as strong, they continue to love. There is no expectation or attachment.

Energy Fields

When two people love each other, there is change at a chemical level and at the energy level — their energy fields change. Both deeply influence each other. So when one has emotions, this can quickly influence the other.

As a Mingjue Gongfu practitioner, you may be in a relationship in which your partner does not know this practice. First, develop a good Mingjue state and trust that Mingjue Love benefits your partner's energy. Do not create conflicts. If your partner creates conflicts, continue cultivating a stable and clear Mingjue state — observe all thoughts, emotions, and sensations, and do not get further entangled. See this as an opportunity to continue to transform yourself and your reference framework, as well as to develop Mingjue. This is the practice in daily life! If you can transform, this means your Mingjue Gongfu has improved.

> Life is the practice ground
> for Mingjue Gongfu.

Mingjue Relationships

Yin and Yang: Feminine and Masculine

At the duality level, males and females appear very different. Their body characteristics reflect into our consciousness and we build a strong reference framework around them. Males have their gender reflected in their reference framework; females have theirs reflected in their reference framework.

In Mingjue Gongfu, we learn to go beyond this duality. Mingjue is the same for both men and women. That is, the feminine Mingjue is a circle containing both yin and yang. The masculine Mingjue is also a circle containing both yin and yang. At this entirety level, individuals are balanced, full, and complete.

This is the Mingjue Love Relationship level. At the levels of physical energy, consciousness, and the reference framework, the complete person remains independent with a full heart. There is no need to control or possess or fear. There is no need for attachment. If you are already in a relationship, you become free and, seemingly paradoxically, you can love the other person more.

At this level, you not only have Mingjue Love, you are Mingjue Love.

Mingjue and Parents

In the Mingjue state, there is love and gratitude toward our parents because Mingjue reflects that they gave us life and that we contain their full life information.

Dr. Pang recognized this. Even in his very full life, he always found time to visit his mother, who lived some six hundred kilometers away. Out of love, gratitude, and respect, he would wash her hair and feet.

Some people may be thinking, "My parents were not good to me when I was young" or, "They were absent from my life." This may be true at the relative level, and in earlier sections on Mingjue Relationships and Emotional Healing, there is information on how to begin to heal and change the information within your consciousness.

When your Mingjue Gongfu is stronger, you can choose to connect to Mingjue Love and have an unconditional relationship with your parents. The past is not important. Just this present moment.

Mingjue and Children

In the Mingjue state, we love our children without attachment and feel the equality between them and us. We do not think that our children belong to us. They are under our care, but are equal with us.

Mingjue and Social Relationships

In relationships with others in society — friends, teachers, students, colleagues, bosses, service workers — it is the same. We relate to them with Mingjue Love and cultivate relationships of equality, gratitude, and respect.

Mingjue and Money

Money is a tool created by people, created by the reference framework of humanity, to acquire material goods and services.

Today, many people struggle for money. This may result from the inequalities that society has created. For others, their struggle may be a desire for more security that they believe comes from more money. Different countries also fight with each other to gain more money or resources. We live in a time of commercial transactions. Even hospitals, schools, and temples have become places of commercial transactions.

How does Mingjue relate to money?

- Mingjue uses money in a free state; it does not attach to or fixate on money. We earn and use money, but do not attach to it.

- Mingjue does not avoid or refuse money. Some may assume that if we practice qigong we do not talk about money. If we attach the labels of "good" or "bad" to money or business, this is another form of fixation. This dualistic thinking can also make us slaves of money.

In China, there is a saying:

The old monk does not like money, but the more the better.

The old monk is a practitioner of Pure Consciousness. Although he may think, "I do not talk about business, I do not need money," he accepts it when people give it to him. In fact, the more, the better, for use toward the common good.

When we are not attached to money, then having money is fine and having no money is also fine. No problem!

As a Mingjue practitioner, we release any and all conflicts with money. We can also choose a simple life. When we have food and shelter, that is enough. We take only what is convenient and necessary for life. When we have less material things, we also have less to become attached to.

Free Mingjue Business

"Free Mingjue Business" means we can earn money without any blockages or fixations on money. Mingjue is considered the most precious resource, so the richness is on the inside.

We can use money as a tool. For example, in addition to meeting our own needs, if we have a lot of money, we can use that money to do something valuable for society. In the Mingjue state, it doesn't matter whether we have a lot of money or no money. We remain free.

A good Mingjue state and healthy Mingjue relationships, however, have the potential to naturally improve our business transactions. We not only become wiser, our energy becomes more beautiful and more powerful, drawing more people to trust in us and do business with us. More opportunities can arise.

So Free Mingjue Business is a high-level business. There is compassion and universal love, which serves us and others alike.

MINGJUE AND THE NATURAL WORLD

Mingjue sends love to the natural world and also receives good information in return. Mingjue Love merges with animals, plants, and flowers.

For example, the moment you see some beautiful flowers and trees, you are already receiving the entirety information in your consciousness. Mingjue receives this beauty and vitality, and the merging can nourish and enhance your life. The relationship between you and the natural world is an entirety. There is no separation. So there is no mindset of wanting to dominate or possess the natural world.

The purer your heart, the more beautiful your eyes can perceive the natural world. By continually focusing on beautiful things and receiving beautiful information, your reference framework will naturally reflect that beauty. Beauty gradually creates harmony and strengthens your inner love.

ON DEATH AND DYING

To fully explore the True Self, whether it is for developing consciousness or for healing, the Mingjue Gongfu student must explore the topic of death. The fear of death is the deepest blockage for most of us, and can create many attachments with our health or relationships that end up controlling us.

If we are attached to life, this can cause fear. If we are attached to death, this can also cause fear.

We actually have a choice in our response and Teacher Wei says, "Choose no fear!" When we practice Mingjue Gongfu, we learn both to observe death and to observe our fear of death — and how to release any attachments to them.

Part of the fear of death is the different cultural frameworks. In many parts of the world, we are sheltered from death. Death feels special and not an ordinary part of life's cycles. In other cultures, however, death is experienced as very ordinary.

Death is not the problem. The fear of death is.

On Your Own Death: You can learn to look directly at death, then see through it. This means to go beyond physical death to the essence of life: qi and consciousness. You can see and experience with clarity and simplicity that life is a journey from birth to death. As a result, you become brave. You can walk with others toward death in a peaceful and free state; even in a state of laughter.

On the Death of Loved Ones: The death of someone you love can be a strong attachment. It is easy for the heart to become distressed or despairing. The ego — your reference framework — may tell you, "You are suffering because you love this person" and, "If you don't suffer, you don't really care." You may be recalling memories of this person. You may remember your beautiful and joyful relationship. Or perhaps you remember some challenges and long for more time to say what you want to say. The more you think and remember, the more you may feel the suffering. This is how the ego and its reference framework operate.

In the same situation, however, you can stay in Mingjue Universal Love and be present with this good information. In doing so, you are sending and receiving good information. This means that Mingjue still contains and retains all the information of the relationship, but the information harmonizes you, inside and out, rather than creating disorder.

So it is, that with the same information of the same experience, we each have a choice of how we might respond — with suffering or harmony.

Death of "I" and "Mine"

Understanding death can influence your life perspective and state, including the process and experience of dying.

As humans, we have two basic fixations or attachments:

1. The Body Ego — the body's nervous system is linked to the sensory organs and the identification of Yiyuanti with the physical body occurs very early in life (see the previous section on Daode Theory for more details). As a result, Yiyuanti can easily become fixated on the physical body — this forms the "body ego." Most of us live our lives with this struggle. We put a lot of effort into our body ego, like keeping our bodies healthy, strong, and beautiful. This includes the food we eat, the clothes we wear, the things we accumulate to add pleasure and beauty to our lives. A strong focus on this can create strife in not wanting to lose the security for the body. And this can create a strong fear of death.

2. The Mind Ego — this refers to the attachment and pride of having accumulated a lot of knowledge. Teacher Wei often hears people say, "I know, I know." Saying or thinking "I know" often reflects the mind ego asserting itself, or perhaps even being offended. "I already know. You do not need to explain," or perhaps, "I know more than you." Or perhaps, some have certain skills, talents, or "super abilities" and want others to know. This is the state of "I" and "mine." This "I" is linked with what we know and also linked with the body. (Usually, when someone says "I," it means his reference framework and body together.) When we have possessions, or in this case, when we possess knowledge, the fixation is that this knowledge is "mine."

Mingjue Gongfu requires that we experience the death of "I" and "mine," of both the body ego and the mind ego, and experience ourselves as one in the collective consciousness field and the Universe Entirety state.

No Death in Mingjue

In Mingjue consciousness, there is no death: in each present moment, as we practice and connect to the collective consciousness field, the perception of death and separation vanishes, and everything is in a constant state of transformation. Therefore, we say there is no death.

Mingjue experiences the physical body. Mingjue experiences the physical body in the process we call life. When the physical body dies, then this particular journey will be complete. When we understand the body as qi or energy, death means the body's energy can no longer function as life. But it remains as qi and converts into another form of energy or existence.

Mingjue observes the birth-death continuum. Both birth and death are concepts within our reference frameworks. Birth is the start of dying and death; death is also a birth of another form of qi existence. Like birth, death is an ordinary phenomenon. In between, the body undergoes different changes from infancy to maturity.

Mingjue observes life in the present moment. The past, future, and present are one in Mingjue. The flow of life is experienced in the "now." The life of the physical body is an ongoing process through time and information, and everyone's physical body will die and transform. This is the law of life. As we come to acceptance, we also come to know that the real meaning and value of life is happening in each present moment.

Mingjue is an entire time-space state. Anyone who remains in this state goes beyond the fixation and fear of death because this state goes beyond the feelings of the body. The feelings are still experienced, but there is no attachment to them. There is also no thinking. This is the independent state.

Mingjue just is. And the present moment is infinite.

Mingjue observes death in the reference framework. The reference framework on death is a tool in the relative dimension. It is neither the total truth nor the conscious observer. Often, people experience the death of the ego as a painful process; this may be associated with physical death and generate some fear.

Different Pathways for Consciousness

Many people want to know what happens after the body dies. Is it final? Or does the soul or consciousness go somewhere? Where is Mingjue?

Different religions have different viewpoints and experiences. Dr. Pang taught some simple information concerning life after death, but did not go into the details. He simply advised his students to focus on the practice, to live well and value each moment. He did not encourage thinking about death or the next life, as it was not useful for gongfu or the state of being.

If we take good care of this life and if there is a next life, said Dr. Pang, the next life will naturally come with good qualities.

TWO BRIEF PRACTICES

If you avoid death or run away from it, the fear remains, even if there is no awareness of it. Here are two practices for you to try:

    1. With your eyes closed, see through to the external world around you. While it may seem like you are directly observing it, you are actually observing the

information within your consciousness. The information of the whole world — the whole universe — is within your consciousness. Your consciousness merges with everything.

2. Practice observing everyday life as just a process and that you are the master observer of its flow. Observe yourself as one cell, undergoing fertilization, growing into a fetus, then a baby, growing up moment by moment, changing in each moment. You can hold the questions, Who am I? Who are we? Are we these bodies? If we are these bodies, then who is observing the body and its changes? Who is the observer? Over time, you can realize the truth about life and also confirm that the observer is the True Self.

Other suggestions: Some Mingjue Gongfu students practice Mingjue and qigong in a cemetery at night. In other traditions, people may lie down in a box to experience lying in a coffin. There are many ways to face death, simulate it, and then go beyond your fears. The most effective way is to gently (and even playfully) train and expose yourself, rather than forcing it or being too tough.

HOW TO DIE WELL

There are ordinary ways to prepare ourselves to die well. There are also special ways.

1. Face and Accept Death — researching about death, observing and facing the death of others can make death a more ordinary and familiar experience. Talking with others about it, attending funerals as they come — gradual exposure is the most gentle way. Not only can your fears diminish, but this can also renew your awareness of the value of life and living in unconditional, universal love.

2. See Through the Life Process — visualizing and observing the process of your own body dying can help to gain a larger perspective of life and death — the macroscopic view.

3. Arrange for Near-Death Care — you can create loving support from your family and friends, and receive support from the collective consciousness field. Both can help cultivate a smooth and easy death.

4. Practice Mingjue. Know that You are an Independent True Self — when you practice Mingjue well, you will naturally know how to die well, because death is a state of universal love. You will know in your whole being, "I am universal love," "I am the master of the energy body." You will face and go beyond death, free and happy. Also, in Mingjue state, there is no death — just transformation of qi. To the very end of your last breath, you can connect to the collective consciousness field and remain the autonomous observer.

Supporting Others at the End of Life

1. Stay in a stable Mingjue state, connected to the collective field.

2. Gather a group of people to support each other — this is even better.

3. Support the consciousness of the person who is dying. When the consciousness field is powerful, transformation can happen.

If someone knows how to practice Mingjue Gongfu but at the end of life his independent Mingjue is not strong enough (and he still attaches to the body and experiences fear), other practitioners can connect with the collective consciousness field and use their Mingjue state to support that person. He can then die in a more independent and harmonious state.

Yi Yuan Ti

SUPER ABILITIES

"Super Abilities" refers to abilities that are beyond the five sensory organs and ordinary knowing. In Mingjue Gongfu, these abilities can develop naturally as the student practices, without necessarily intending to develop them. This is because Mingjue is the master of information and also the master of itself. It reflects all the information it receives. So sometimes, this information may express as images or sounds or smells. Other times, there is just direct knowing.

Super abilities describe two functions of Mingjue:

1. Receiving Information — Mingjue can receive information in two general ways:

• Ordinary abilities — this kind of information comes through the five sensory organs. It is partial information built on the ordinary reference framework.

• Super abilities — this kind of information comes directly and completely to Mingjue, and not through the five sensory organs or ordinary thinking. Sometimes this is called paranormal abilities; others know it as extrasensory perceptions. Examples of super abilities include:

1- Hearing sounds from five thousand kilometers away

2- Seeing through matter, like seeing inside someone else's body

2. Sending Information — Mingjue can also send information in the two general ways (ordinary and super abilities). An example of this is Mingjue Healing.

Direct Change, Direct Knowing

Dr. Pang often said that speaking is also a practice — a high-level practice. That is, the information contained in the theories is also a form of transformation if the listener is open and trusting. When the teacher speaks and the information rings true to the students and they internally have a realization or awakening, this is another form of direct change. Sometimes the direct change can happen without a clear understanding; this is how transmissions work.

The potential for super abilities comes when Mingjue receives information about itself. When Mingjue receives self-information, it stays in the Mingjue state and becomes very stable. Over time, the information of Mingjue itself becomes the central information.

So when we practice, we need to repeat the self-information of Mingjue over and over again. This repetition is not a form of thinking — it is an observation. At the same time, we can feel universal love and allow this information to also become part of the central information.

Two Life Systems

Dr. Pang described the following Two Life Systems. When we practice Zhineng Qigong, we primarily practice the Second Life System. But to live a complete life, we must integrate the Second Life System with the First Life System.

1. First Life System: Prevailing Framework

Consciousness makes decisions through the five sensory organs, through the body's physiological systems.

2. Second Life System: Consciousness Information Decides the Life State

Super abilities belong to this Second Life System.

Consciousness directly sends information to make changes in the body (bypasses the nervous system).

Consciousness also sends information to itself, so it changes itself.

MINGJUE AND SUPER ABILITIES

Most humans only use ~10% of their brains. If just 5-10% more is activated, someone's life state can readily and dramatically change.

Super Abilities Outside of Mingjue

Someone who doesn't know Mingjue consciousness can also develop super abilities. For example, if someone practices the Open Heavenly Gate method, or does Open/Close or La Qi on the Upper Dantian, super abilities can still appear. The difference is that the practitioner is not aware that he is the observer.

At this level, the super abilities can be used to improve consciousness, to arrive at the Mingjue level. If Mingjue consciousness is not developed, the super abilities become blocked energy at a certain level; the student cannot improve beyond that. Without Mingjue consciousness, the student also risks using the super abilities for his own human will — even good will — and this can become a fixation in the reference framework, strengthening the ego personality.

Super abilities without Mingjue consciousness also risk having the practitioner feel "special." This can also limit the life state.

The reality: everybody has access to Mingjue — it is the collective consciousness field where we are all one! That means everybody can develop Mingjue functions. So when we experience super abilities, we must realize that we are experiencing everyone else's potential. This keeps pride from becoming an obstruction.

> Without Mingjue state,
> super abilities can become
> a super ego.

Note: The super abilities reference framework is more expanded than the ordinary framework; but Mingjue ability is higher and purer.

At the Mingjue level, super abilities are a function of Mingjue and can support Mingjue to improve.

FOUR PRINCIPLES TO TRUST IN DEVELOPING SUPER ABILITIES

1. Know that everything is qi.

2. Your consciousness can transform qi. Do you really trust that your mind can make your body qi change? Do you trust the theories and concepts? Or do you trust from your inner experience? The former is a good first step, but the latter is important for real change.

3. Trust that your consciousness has great potential awaiting you.

4. Trust that you can develop and unlock the potential of your consciousness.

The Life of a Sage

Sage: a complete and peaceful person with wisdom and compassion.

A sage has the following characteristics:

• A sage's essence is to know and be the awakening self, or True Self. This is self-knowledge.

• A sage is peaceful, free, happy, and harmonious. Their state are very stable.

• A sage has deep compassion and universal love.

• A sage is wise and always remains in the Mingjue Entirety state. The sage wants to benefit the entirety. They have big heart.

• A sage is selfless and without attachments.

When we think of sages, our consciousness connects with their high-level information. We can then learn from them — their knowledge, practice, and the state of their consciousness — and merge and be one with them.

Examples of Sages:

- Laozi, the founder of Daoism, whose state was one with the universe.

- Buddha, who highlighted the awakening state and great compassion.

- Jesus, who emphasized universal love and awakening universal love.

- Confucius, who taught universal love and harmony in human society.

- Bodhidharma, an important sage for the Chinese Zen Buddhist culture.

- Wang Yangming, a man who achieved enlightenment five hundred years ago and did many beneficial things for society. He knew his time of death and said, "My heart is bright and has reached awakening. That is enough for this life. I need nothing else." Then he died in a peaceful state.

From Dr. Pang: "If you want to be a high-level person, you need to think that you already are that. Then you will feel and act accordingly."

In other words, quietly visualize and observe a small Buddha or Christ or True Self within you. This is subtle. It is important not to draw a line between you and the sages. This separation creates an attitude of worship and a distance between you and the collective field.

On the opposite end, if you feel strongly or tell others things like, "I am a Buddha!" or, "I am the True Self!" this categorically does not come from Mingjue state and will create blockages and more separation.

Suggested Practice: You may try to think and visualize, "I am Dr. Pang" or, "Dr. Pang's consciousness is in me, and mine is in him." "My hands are Dr. Pang's hands." You can merge with his consciousness in the collective field, experience his big heart and awakening state, and receive his high-level information and harmonious state to transform your inner state and old conditioned habits.

Six Levels of Knowing

1. Yiyuanti reflects itself — this is Mingjue (also called lingjue 灵觉) — a very pure level of knowing that springs forth from the origin. This is a **natural enlightenment**, meaning a natural awakened state that contains everything in oneness.

2. Yiyuanti reflects the existence of things, knows the existence of things in a simple way. For example, Yiyuanti reflects the existence of the physical body, the house, the natural world. Judgment has not yet appeared. Nor have any fixations.

3. Yiyuanti knows when things occur, and which experiences are good or bad for life. At this level, judgment appears but as simple reactions. For example, a toddler sees fire, touches it, experiences pain, and then judges it as "bad."

4. Yiyuanti can make moral judgments and determine the qualities of a moral or immoral person. At this level, logical thinking strongly appears. This knowing gradually departs further and further from the source of Yiyuanti.

5. Yiyuanti can know and judge concepts linked with science, the arts, the news, and other frameworks. The reach of Yiyuanti expands more into the external world. Every day, the mind receives waves of information from the external world, becoming busy in making judgments about all kinds of information.

6. Sage Level — Yiyuanti reflects itself, remains in Mingjue state, and simultaneously knows things at all the other levels. Sages always remain in the centered Mingjue Entirety state. They know they judge, but there is no fixation to the judgment. It is a free and neutral judgment — a discernment. Sages may guide or point the way to the wise path, but they do so without criticism or blame. They know that everyone, at their origin, is the True Self with a pure baby heart and that confusion and disagreements come from the reference frameworks. Sages also guide without praise. Rather, with compassion. This is different from the "natural enlightenment" (Level 1 above), because this is an **awakened enlightenment.**

BECOMING A SAGE

Everyone and anyone can become a sage. Inside our hearts, a sage is already there, even if we have attachments and fixed ideas, even if we aren't aware of the inner sage. When we practice Zhineng Qigong and Mingjue Gongfu, the intention is to become a sage. Dr. Pang used to say that the practice of Zhineng Qigong is the transformation of the sick into a sage.

The foundation of the sage is the **pure baby heart**. The baby heart reflects our thoughts and also the external world. Once the baby heart awakens, it begins to consciously grow and develop.

Our inner sage is Mingjue. The function of Mingjue is what creates the behaviors of a sage. This means that the sage's inner work is to receive information in the Mingjue state.

Reflection Questions:

- What kind of person do you want to be in this life?

- Having experienced worldly life, have you found that worldly desires can bring joy, but can also create problems?

- Who is choosing to rise to a higher level and experience something new?

PART 2: METHODS AND PRACTICES

The methods and practices in this section focus on Mingjue consciousness and breath work. For specific guidelines on dynamic (movement) methods beyond the foundational Mingjue Gongfu practices, please refer to Dr. Pang Ming's books (The Methods of Zhineng Qigong Science *and* Later Methods Zhineng Qigong and Taiji) *as well as instructional videos from The World Consciousness Community.*

All of these can be found at www.theworldconsciousnesscommunity.com

EVERYDAY READINGS

Complete Version

We are Mingjue

> *I love you*

> > *You love me*

> > > *We love each other*

> > > > *Heart to heart*

> > > > > *We are one.*

Practice Mingjue Entirety diligently, with good self-discipline.

Make a beautiful life and family with Mingjue love.

Build a powerful consciousness field

to bring awakening, peace, and happiness to the world.

Simplified Version

I am Mingjue love

> *I love me*

> *I love us*

> > *We are Mingjue love*

> *We love me*

We love us

> *We love the world.*

PRACTICING AS A COMMUNITY

In The World Consciousness Community, we practice in a collective way, rooted in universal love. Smaller communities support each other to strengthen relationships and connection. Then the smaller communities connect together to form a strong collective consciousness field. In actuality, the small and big communities are one.

This is different from practitioners who learn by themselves, often changing from teacher to teacher or taking a variety of courses. This is in large part due to the lack of community strength and intimacy.

Discipline and Devotion. To experience change, your practice must be at the center of your life. Without regular practice, you cannot develop a good understanding or gongfu of the methods. Only through consistent practice will consciousness become steadily more concentrated, pure, stable, and powerful. As a consequence, your qi and physical body will change more, as will your overall lifestyle. Training is necessary to have a high-level quality of life.

Fewer, Deeper. Teacher Wei practiced and taught qigong for 30 years and learned many methods. He found that when people practiced just a few simple methods for a longer period of time, they experienced good improvements. If they practice many different methods and also different traditions — a little yoga, some taiji, other qigong lineages — the information could cause divisions in their consciousness and their qi could become scattered and disordered.

This is like making a well to find water under the earth: it's more effective to focus on one general area, dig, and go deeper and deeper. Eventually, the water will be discovered. If someone always changes the locations of digging and doesn't go deeper, he will never find the water.

So choose a few methods and go deep.

Practicing With and Without Guidance. Teacher Wei recommends practicing with live and recorded guidance to develop a good, basic foundation of the Mingjue Entirety state. Then once the foundation is there, from time to time, practice by your own inner guidance. This can reduce the risk of becoming attached to the methods, the teacher(s), and/or the physical or emotional sensations.

KEY ENERGY GATES AND POINTS

Important Energy Points, Channels, Palaces, and Dantians

Energy points are places where qi goes in and out from qi channels. Channels are columns of qi. Dantians are large centers or spaces of qi. Palaces are smaller centers or spaces of qi.

1. **Huiyin** — this energy point sits in the perineal area. From the skin of the perineum, it is about 3-4 cm upward. Ideally, Huiyin is gently lifted up and closed, and remains so, to reduce energy leakage. This is a yin energy point — meaning it relates to the feminine energy that flows downward.

2. **Baihui** — this energy point sits at the crown of the head. It is a yang energy point — which is masculine energy that flows upward.

3. **Middle Channel** (also called Central Channel) — this energy column runs along the central axis of the body. It is a straight line that connects the Huiyin at the perineum and the Baihui at the crown of the head. Through this channel, yin and yang connect together.

4. **Duqi** (pronounced "doo chee") — this point is at the navel (belly button). It serves as the portal through which developing fetuses gathered energy while in the mother's womb. After birth, Duqi is an energy gate that connects external qi and consciousness; it also connects innate and acquired qi. Acquired qi gathers behind Duqi in the abdomen.

5. **Mingmen** (Gate of Life) — this point is located at the lumbar spine (L2-3), directly opposite Duqi. Mingmen Inner Palace is the empty space just anterior to Mingmen that, as a complement to the acquired qi of Duqi, contains innate qi, or very concentrated genetic information. In Zhineng Qigong, there are many practices from Mingmen.

6. **Shenji Palace** — this energy space is in the center of the Upper Dantian in the head. The pineal gland is at its center.

7. **Yintang** — this energy point sits between the eyebrows. It is a direct line anterior from the Shenji Palace. Many have mistakenly believed this point to be the "third eye." The third eye, however, is located in the pineal gland, or Shenji Palace.

8. **Shanzhong** — this energy point sits on the anterior chest between the nipples.

9. **Dumai** — this big qi channel runs along the spine. Methods that improve the flexibility of the spine opens the flow of this channel.

10. **Renmai** — this big qi channel runs along the anterior (front) side of the body.

11. **Hun Yuan Palace** — this energy space sits between the Middle and Lower Dantians, below the diaphragm, in and around the pancreas. It connects with both the lower and Middle Dantian qi. There is a strong qi field in and around the pancreas area because of the continuous movement of the diaphragm (the breath). Hun Yuan Palace is also called Hun Yuan Qiao. This is where the qi of the lungs and heart descends and merges with the qi of the pancreas, liver, and kidneys. So it is the qi center of the five inner organs system.

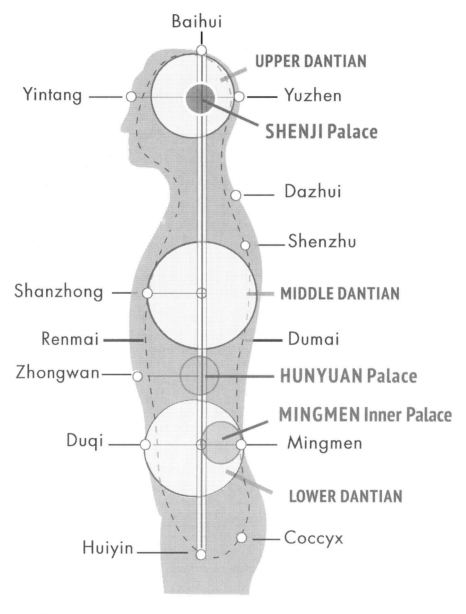

The Five Inner Organs System and Hun Yuan Palace

In Middle and Lower Dantian (chest and abdomen), there are five inner organ systems: heart, kidneys, pancreas/spleen, liver, and lungs. The Hun Yuan Palace is where the pure qi of these five organ systems converge. This qi is responsible for the hormones of the body and relates to our emotions. This qi is purer than that of the Lower Dantian (inner bodily Hun Yuan Qi), but not as fine as the qi of the Upper Dantian.

The Three Energy Centers: Dantians

1. Lower Dantian

This is a large energy center in the abdomen between Duqi (navel) and Mingmen ("gate of life"). In the diagram above, there is a circle; this is not an actual circle, but a representation of the space.

When we eat or drink, nourishment is transformed into energy, and this acquired qi is stored in this space. In the diagram, the Lower Dantian encompasses another important space called **Mingmen Inner Palace** (a special energy space reviewed above). Since Mingmen Inner Palace contains innate or genetic qi, the Lower Dantian is the space where acquired and innate qi merge together.

The function of Lower Dantian qi is to nourish and develop the cells of the physical body. Lower Dantian qi is the energy required for growth and the daily transformation of the body and its cells. Lower Dantian qi also supplies the energy for all physical movements. For instance, carrying heavy loads, walking, talking, and laughing.

Lower Dantian qi is called **bodily Hun Yuan Qi**. This qi is rougher or denser in quality than Upper Dantian qi.

2. Middle Dantian

This energy center is located in the chest space. The qi of the Middle Dantian is the qi field of the heart, lungs, and breasts. The qi field in the chest is cultivated by the continuous movements of the heart, lungs, and diaphragm, and is very powerful.

3. Upper Dantian

This energy center is located in the head. It is formed by the qi of the brain cells merging together and forming a strong qi center. Upper Dantian qi is primarily used for the activity of consciousness. It is necessary for any mental activity.

Upper Dantian qi is finer in quality than that of the Lower and Middle Dantians — it is **similar in quality to the purest and finest qi of the Original Hun Yuan Qi**. So the qi of Upper Dantian can readily merge with universal qi.

PRACTICE: SETTING A GOOD CONSCIOUSNESS ENTIRETY FIELD

Sit up straight, gently lifting up the Baihui (the crown of the head), your feet planted on the floor. Soften your gaze.

Draw consciousness into Shenji Palace (the center of your head). From Shenji Palace, observe the head inner space. The inner space of the head is even and pure.

Observe the whole body inside, and continue observing it. Observe the subtle space. The whole body inside becomes even and pure.

Observe the universal space around you — the inner space merges with the universal space. It becomes even and pure, very harmonious, very peaceful.

In the universal space, your consciousness state merges together with all the other practitioners' and teachers' states, heart to heart. Experience this beautiful consciousness field.

This consciousness field merges with all the subtle spaces inside your qi body. This consciousness field supports your consciousness, improving and supporting your qi to transform and become purer.

This collective consciousness field transforms and purifies the information and energy field of the whole world.

Feel that your consciousness and the entire high-level consciousness field are one.

Deep inside, send this information to yourself: throughout our collective Mingjue Gongfu practice, everybody's consciousness, qi, and body will improve to a high level and good healing state. Our daily lives, behaviors and all of our relationships become more harmonious. We have more abilities and wisdom to handle all kinds of things in the best possible way.

Maintaining this peaceful state, open your eyes slowly.

Try to maintain this state and to keep this information in your awareness throughout your day and night.

FOUR KEY PRACTICES FOR IMPROVING MINGJUE GONGFU

Mingjue Gongfu is developed through **four key practices**, each one significant on its own, but interrelated with the others:

1. Observation
2. Concentration
3. Relaxation
4. Transformation

OBSERVATION

If consciousness cannot be seen, heard, or felt through the five senses, how can you know the state of your consciousness? The only way is for consciousness to observe itself.

The power of observation requires conscious training. When you observe the body internally, your consciousness goes throughout the interior space. **Only after you become proficient in observation can you effectively engage in the practice of the other methods.**

Observation - Guan Cha

In Mingjue Gongfu training, you learn to connect to your inner observer — this observer observes all the sensations, experiences, and movements of qigong practice. When you observe a specific internal space, you receive information from that place. The more relaxed and focused the observation, the deeper the awareness of that place.

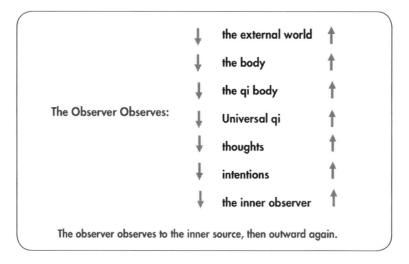

The Observer Observes:

↓ the external world ↑

↓ the body ↑

↓ the qi body ↑

↓ Universal qi ↑

↓ thoughts ↑

↓ intentions ↑

↓ the inner observer ↑

The observer observes to the inner source, then outward again.

Observation in Different Situations

1. When **observing the material world** (before we come to the Mingjue state), we naturally attach to the material world, occupy the material world, and live confined to the material world. This is how we become enslaved to the material world and why we experience a lot of fear.

2. When **observing others**, our minds become occupied with them. We develop affection, conditional love, and often suffer as a result. We become dependent on them.

3. When **observing the body** we naturally attach to the body and its sensations. We can fixate on its appearance, shape, or on beauty and health. We can fixate on the body, or fear death and dying. But we can also learn to observe energy from the external world returning to nourish the body.

4. When **observing qi**, we may feel alive or powerful. Observing qi can make our lives healthier and stronger. We can also go further beyond the physical body, to experience the qi of the universe — thus having more freedom and harmony. It can be easy to fixate on qi and also fixate on the feeling of emptiness.

5. When **observing thoughts**, we can fixate on the ego or on the ideas of the self. We can also fixate on knowledge. This can block our gongfu. But we can go deeper within, returning to the realm of consciousness. Then we can see through our mind and learn to manage our thoughts in daily life.

6. When **observing the reference framework**, we may see different patterns or fixed beliefs. The inner programming can start to upgrade, but we can also become fixated on that.

7. When *intentionally* **observing the observer**, we allow the Mingjue state to appear. This state goes beyond all the other attachments. Now we just come to ourselves, to the True Self. We attain freedom, peace, and unconditional love. This is still not the deepest state, because an intention remains. In the end, when we come to the True Self, the intention disappears.

8. When *unintentionally* **observing the observer**, we have reached a state of **reflection, enlightenment, or Being**. We experience the essence of ourselves, Yiyuanti, "Buddha nature," True Nature. Dr. Pang called it "lingyuan" (灵元) or True Self. There are many other names for this "I am" state.

Observing Different Levels in the Body

When we observe, we need to experience not only the surface of our bodies, but all the different layers and dimensions, down to the qi level. For example, if we observe the eyes, we go beyond the surface of eyes to observing the outer and inner layers like a transparent space.

This transparent space is like a clear crystal. We can see through crystals. In the body, the "crystal" isn't a physical, dense space. It is a transparent, empty space, flowing and vibrating.

For example, when you observe the heart, start at the surface, then penetrate through the inner layers. You may know the shape of the heart, so when you observe it with your inner eye, you immediately see the image of the heart inside your body. But don't stop there. Go deeper to directly observe the entire space of the heart — the crystal — down to the heart organ as pure qi. The transparent qi permeates the totality of the heart from the surface to deep inside its center. Feel the vibration of that space, the flow of qi.

When this level of observation occurs in your consciousness, an experience will emerge of the inner qi space that permeates all material things (matter) — meaning you will train your power of observation to observe the essence of the living universe around you, as well as within.

As you observe this way, a change will happen in the places you observe. How big a change depends on how powerful and pure your observer is. This is why, **in and of itself, observation can be a very effective form of healing.**

The more deeply you can observe within, the more easily your consciousness can let go of external attachments and fixations. When Teacher Wei says, "**Observe but not observe**" or, "**Do not observe but observe**," this means that, although the intention is still there, it is all but disappeared.

Note: When Teacher Wei says to observe the inner space of a particular body part (example: the spine or the chest), this is both passive and active — passivity and activity are one, meaning that you receive information at the same time you experience the inner qi space of that body part. If your consciousness is not sufficiently clear, you will only be passive. With a clear consciousness, you can clearly perceive the experience of activity, and the passive and active states become one. There is no longer a distinction between passive or active.

High-level awareness: Sometimes Mingjue Gongfu students may feel the state of emptiness, but they may not be aware that the emptiness is their consciousness. Only when the observer comes to itself — knows itself — only at that moment can the emptiness and consciousness become one. It is as though the empty space awakens.

CONCENTRATION

Concentration means that your consciousness can focus on one state, one place, without anything else, for increasingly longer periods of time. This is basic gongfu. Without good training, concentration remains limited. Many people practice

Concentration - Zhuan Zhu

for many years, and yet their qigong level does not improve. This is due to an insufficient ability to concentrate; their consciousness does not have enough power.

In static meditation methods, you can train to go deeply within. Consciousness can merge with the qi body, continually going deeper and deeper. You can also train your concentration while lying down before sleep, and sleep in the state in which consciousness observes and merges with the qi body. In this state, you think of nothing else.

Ru-ding: *Ding* means a state of stability. It means staying in one harmonious state without fixation or attachment. *Ru-ding* means to go into a very stable, pure state for a long time. Students will naturally go beyond time and space — meaning they lose the sense of time and space and forget everything.

Ru Ding

Students can arrive at the ru-ding state when the observer observes one place in the qi body, Mingjue merges with the qi of that space, and this entirety becomes very stable. In the ru-ding state, 30 minutes, one hour, or two hours can feel like 10 minutes.

If your ding power is not strong, you can continuously lose yourself or bring yourself problems.

Two Examples of Ding Power

• With fighters, someone may fight with others while his internal state remains peaceful and pure. That's ding power.

• If someone is being attacked by hateful words but is not influenced by the information, this is ding power, too.

You can begin to train this power during less stressful times, maintaining the purest consciousness state with stability. Then, add a little challenge by practicing standing meditation while remaining in this pure state. Then, add some dynamic methods while staying in this state. Then, communicate with others and notice if their ideas or emotional states can influence you. If other people argue, are you angry? Can you stay in the group and keep a peaceful, stable, and relaxed state?

This ability gives you the potential to change the qi and information of others and bring benefit to the environment.

RELAXATION

When you enter a qi state, you naturally relax. Relaxation manifests in your consciousness and body.

The relaxation of consciousness requires that you become very pure internally. There are no attachments. There is no excitement. Relaxation helps you to go deeper and open up to transformation.

Relaxation
Fang Song

TRANSFORMATION

When consciousness is focused and stable, transformation will naturally occur as it travels inwardly. Once the information is given, transformation will occur. When consciousness goes to a very subtle level in the deep inner space of the qi body, **transformation happens at the same time as observation**.

Remember that your life is the practice, too! Train your mind to feel and experience the complete entirety state, always — while walking, running, driving the car, doing housework, in your relationships and in your work.

This state is one of energy conservation; you will lose a lot less qi to external triggers or distractions.

This state is also one of energy increase; you can also naturally gather more universal qi inside of you and produce more internal qi. You do not need to think about it — it will happen naturally!

Transformation
Zhuan Hua

At a very deep level of Mingjue state, the body's energy is very balanced and harmonious. Problems transform and disappear.

Consciousness contains all the information of humanity and the universe, so you have everything you need. It is as if a "universe creator" exists within everyone's consciousness and has the potential to create a beautiful consciousness state there.

> Transformation follows
> the information.

Generally, we live our lives with consciousness separated from the body; we do not think of our body's deep inner space. Our minds can be hundreds of miles away, or in the past or future. Many physical, emotional, and mental challenges are created by this separation of body and consciousness.

Mingjue Gongfu provides simple movements that aim to:

- Open your inner space to experience harmony and happiness

- Integrate consciousness and body

- Open the body structure to build the body's entirety, improve flexibility, and increase flow

- Improve the ability of consciousness to control the body

- Improve health internal qi is abundant and flows freely; functions are wonderful

High-Level Mingjue Practice

In Mingjue Gongfu, the foundation of all practices — including the dynamic (movement) methods — is to first develop a good Mingjue state. Mingjue merges with the qi body and goes beyond it, merging with the collective consciousness field and the universal qi field. Then, while in this Mingjue Entirety state, the dynamic methods are practiced slowly, gently. This entirety state is what makes this a high-level practice. Practicing all the movements and methods in this entirety is not easy. You must train in order to practice well.

> Where consciousness goes, qi follows.

A Note on Static and Dynamic Methods

The gaze. In the beginning of the practices that follow, it says to "soften the gaze." This is because you are reading the words to learn or understand the practice. In actuality, these practices are deepened by closing your eyes. Once you are familiar with the practices, you can practice on your own or practice to an audio recording with your eyes closed.

Most dynamic methods not included in this book. Since it is difficult to learn dynamic methods through text alone (it is much easier by video or audio recording or live practice), only the simplest dynamic methods are included here. The dynamic methods Teacher Wei teaches in the Mingjue Gongfu courses include but are not limited to: Caterpillar Movement, Big Circulation, Bow Body/Arch

Back, Chen Qi, Hip Rotations, Lower Spine Rotations, Push/Pull, and Crane's Head. Please refer to Teacher Wei's recordings at The World Consciousness Community. Or if you're interested to see them in text format with illustrations, please refer to Dr. Pang's books.

Dr. Pang on practicing dynamic methods: "When you practice Lift Qi Up, concentrate on consciousness doing the movement, and do not think about the flow of qi. This is the high-level practice."

"When you do the movement Push/Pull, your Mingjue consciousness is in the universe as you push, and consciousness is in the body as you pull." In this way, consciousness becomes very light because you carry nothing. Qi naturally follows consciousness, so you do not need to think about gathering qi. If you think about qi and drawing in qi, it will feel heavy."

Trust this principle: you do not need to draw in qi. Rather, qi will follow your consciousness. **All movements are Mingjue movements. All movements are about you coming into your True Self.**

FOUNDATIONAL PRACTICE: TRAINING THE OBSERVER

Key Points

- Go through and beyond form/matter.

- Create the experience of inner qi space.

- Experience emptiness.

- Experience the movement of qi in the inner space.

- Go to a deeper and subtler level.

- Mingjue is a state of Pure Consciousness where the inner observer observes itself, and then becomes self-aware.

[Please review Repeating the Shenji Sound and Repeating the ñ Sound in the subsequent section, Sound Practices, as foundations for this practice.]

Note: This practice can be done saying Shenji or ñ. To improve Mingjue, the primary practice is to say ñ.

Sit up straight, gently lifting up the Baihui (the crown of the head), your feet planted on the floor. Soften your gaze.

Say ñ… ñ… ñ…. Draw your mind into Shenji Palace. Relax.

Focus finer and finer inside Shenji Palace. Now observe the head inner space. Observe the inside of your head becoming pure and even.

Gradually draw your focus downward, observing the neck's inner space. Feel how qi is flowing inside this space. Can you observe and feel the qi moving and flowing inside?

Observe the inner space of the shoulders and arms. The arms are empty space, very pure.

Now observe the inner space of the chest. Go through the lungs. How deep, how fine a level can you observe down into each space? Feel how relaxed you are.

Observe throughout the breasts. Go through the transparent space, deeper and deeper.

This is basic Mingjue Gongfu. If you can observe qi on very subtle levels, you can come to observe Pure Consciousness as well.

Observe the heart's inner space. Go throughout that space, stay inside and relax some more. Sleep within the inner space of the chest.

Relaxation: If you don't feel empty enough, relax your consciousness more and more — until you are "asleep but not asleep." The more relaxed you are, the finer and emptier you become inside. If you feel the internal spaces of any particular body part as tense or blocked, observe throughout the inner deepest layers of that space; that space then becomes empty.

Concentration: If you do not feel focused enough, you can silently say Shenji and, at the same time, observe the inner space of the specific body part. Allow the memory of your physical body, which comes from the sensory organs, to disappear. Focus on the emptiness within, smaller and smaller, infinitesimally smaller.

Now use the Pure Consciousness state of Mingjue to go through the whole body in this same manner. This is different than recognizing sensations from sensory organs. Pure Consciousness is just pure qi; it goes through the subtler internal levels. When you go through the different layers of the body, the internal qi is changed — transformed.

Observe the inner space of the abdomen.

Observe throughout the liver and gallbladder.

Observe throughout stomach and intestines.

Observe throughout the pancreas and spleen.

Observe throughout the kidneys.

Observe the bladder and reproductive system.

Observe the whole Lower Dantian space in the inner space of the abdomen.

Observe the inner space of the legs, hips, thighs, knees, calves, ankles, and feet.

Observe the spine's inner space. Go slowly through the cervical vertebrae, thoracic, lumbar, and tailbone. Observe the whole spine's inner space.

The whole body is pure qi.

Empty more.

Relax more.

Observe the whole qi body.

Feel consciousness merging with the whole qi body, becoming one — like a fine, fine mist filling the emptiness of the qi body.

Observe inside deeper and deeper. This focused but light observation can make great changes in your body.

Say ñ softly. Note the vibration happening in Shenji Palace. At the same time, since consciousness is merged with the entire qi body, the vibration also happens in the internal space of the body. Shenji Palace is therefore the center of the whole body.

The more deeply you observe, the more peace, harmony, and happiness you will naturally come to feel as a side-effect of this practice.

When you finish this practice, continuously think ñ and stay connected to Shenji Palace throughout your daily life.

PRACTICE: OBSERVING UPPER DANTIAN AND SHENJI PALACE

With a smile on the face, gently relax your gaze. Feel your consciousness return to Shenji Palace, deep inside the head. Feel your consciousness return to the present moment. Mind nothing else.

Staying inside Shenji Palace, softly say ñ. Give an inner smile within Yintang's inner space (posterior to the Yintang energy point between the eyebrows). Your smile goes from that space to Shenji Palace and fills the whole Upper Dantian space. Observe the pure emptiness inside Shenji Palace and Upper Dantian — it is a very pure emptiness. Relax your observation so you are "observing but not observing." Notice how the Upper Dantian space becomes a pure space, transparent and bright. This brightness has no color or light. However, if you experience color or light in the head, it does not matter; notice how there is another level where there is no light. It is pure emptiness, but it is a bright emptiness — "bright emptiness" does not mean light, but clear like a crystal. Your consciousness and this pure emptiness are crystal clear.

Observe the deep interior of the Upper Dantian. Relax within this space. With continued practice, you begin to experience the empty space of Shenji Palace and the empty space of the universe as one — all boundaries disappear.

Observe your intention. There should be just a very slight intention guiding the practice. This subtle intention comes from pure information.

Observe the pure space of the universe and your Pure Consciousness merging with one another. This is Teacher Wei's information; it is also your information. This information becomes a gentle intention — simply that you feel the high-level collective field merging together with your Pure Consciousness — and reminds you that we are one. The world consciousness field becomes stronger and stronger. Trust this reality. Directly experience this reality.

There is no need to judge, as these things are so subtle. When you have the powerful gongfu of observation, you will naturally see and experience this unified reality inside. And the more you know this pure level of reality through direct experience, the greater your life transforms. The vibration of your entire life will happen at a higher level.

Stay in the present moment — always.

PRACTICE: OBSERVING YIYUANTI

With a smile on the face, gently relax your gaze. Draw consciousness back to Shenji Palace in the center of your head.

Visualize the qi of the brain cells and observe the inner space of the brain cells inside the head. The pure qi of the brain cells connects together. It is very fine, very even. Observe.

When you are just beginning this practice, it is more of a visualization. Continue to observe, observe, and observe. You will come to realize this as a reality.

Observe the fine qi of the brain cells as a big, invisible mirror that reflects deep inside.

Now it reflects the inner space of the earth.

The heavens.

The whole universe — the empty space of the whole qi universe.

It also reflects itself.

Observation is one of the functions of Yiyuanti — it is a form of receiving information. So when you observe the qi universe, you are receiving the information of universe and come to know its essence. And you have merged with the qi universe.

Now observe the inner space of the head. Yiyuanti can choose to gather into the head's inner space. Observe the head's inner space — it is Yiyuanti receiving the information from that space and reflecting it, so you can clearly come to know the head's inner space.

Now observe the inner space of the neck, realizing it is Yiyuanti that is receiving information about the neck's inner space and reflecting it back to you.

Now, the inner space of the whole body, part by part. Yiyuanti clearly reflects the subtle levels.

This is how you can train Yiyuanti to guide your observation gongfu. Through observation as a practice, you come to know the existence of Yiyuanti by its function.

After you have observed the qi body part by part, place your palms on Duqi. Feel the breathing of your big qi body.

Separate the hands to the sides. Slowly restore your gaze.

Homework

Review Yiyuanti Theory in Part I: Theory. Then practice observing on your own while sitting, lying down, or in Standing Meditation. There is a lot of information. So review it often, digest it, absorb it, and then experience it.

PRACTICING OBSERVATION IN DAILY LIFE

1. Find a few times during your day to practice observing the empty spaces of your qi body, part by part. Set an alarm if it's useful.

2. At night before you sleep, repeat ñ... ñ... ñ.... As you make the sounds, observe your inner body becoming empty. Observe and expand this empty space from the center of the head. Gradually observe and expand this empty space to the neck, then methodically down your body, down to the feet and toes. Observe the whole body as empty. Then your consciousness merges and harmonizes with the qi body. If you train this way every night, you may see that you can go deeper and emptier with increasing ease.

3. Going Deeper: Observing the qi body is an effective practice for staying in the present moment. But this is only going halfway. To heal and awaken more, practice observing your emotions, your thoughts, and the origin of the thoughts. Where are the thoughts coming from? And who is observing the thoughts and emotions? Observe the reference framework and observe any memories that surface, going into and through them. Eventually, the observer comes to observe itself — becomes aware of its awareness — and suddenly the path opens, like an opening from earth to heaven.

4. A simple practice: Mingjue observes itself as a clear crystal and says, "I AM... I AM... I AM..."

Three Ways to Improve the Power of the Observer

1. Observe the sound ñ or Shenji — focus.

2. Observe the breath — go through and merge with the whole qi body.

3. Observe the movements — practice the movements with the observer and your breath leading them.

Reflection Questions

Take some time to answer the following questions. By simply asking them, they become your intention and help you deepen your experiences. If you don't have the answers yet, keep practicing! You can come into the answers through your practice.

1. How deep and fine can you observe Shenji Palace? Your Mingmen Inner Palace? What is your experience?

2. When you have tension in your consciousness and/or body, how do you relax there? How do you transform the tension into emptiness?

3. If you have problems in the body, how can you observe and transform them?

4. Can you feel your observation becoming more stable?

5. What is the experience of your qi body breathing?

6. How do you know when you are in Mingjue state? (When you are thinking that you are in Mingjue state, are you?)

BREATHING PRACTICES OVERVIEW

Key Points

- Qi Entirety, observation, concentration, relaxation

- Expansion

- Hunhua (merging and transforming)

In Zhineng Qigong, "breathing" does not refer only to the movement of air through the nose and lungs. Primarily, breathing refers to the movement of qi (Qi Body Breathing). When the nose and lungs are breathing, qi movement happens in and throughout the whole body and within all the cells.

Qi Body Breathing can also occur through the skin (Skin Breathing), with qi moving in and out of the skin, all around the body, with each inhalation and exhalation. Qi Body Breathing requires training.

While breathing practices are at **the Second Entirety level of practice — where the body and consciousness serve qi** — they can help you to deepen your awareness of consciousness within. And if you hold the awareness, who is observing the breath and who is initiating the breath, you will be practicing the **Third Entirety level of practice, where the body and qi serve consciousness.**

Three Important Points for Breathing Practices

- Focus on your breath to create a kind of qi feeling. But remember that the qi body feeling is a short-lived phenomenon that will eventually disappear.

- **A secret from Teacher Wei:** When you connect your breathing to a particular place in your body, the breathing movements will mobilize the energy there. **It will seem as though the breathing is happening within and from that place.** If you focus in the spine, for example, your consciousness will create the feeling of breathing in the spine. That is, your consciousness will draw the support of the breath to mobilize your spine's inner qi.

- Keep in mind that the primary purpose of these practices is **to enhance your power of observation**. By focusing on your breath, you are consciously observing deeper, and with more focus and relaxation. If your only purpose is to observe the breath, you are overlooking the purpose of training the power of observation, and your power of observation can then diminish. The whole point of all these practices is to strengthen the ability of your consciousness.

Two Styles of Breathing Practices

Strong: Throat Breathing, or holding the breath — the air goes through the nose and lungs fast and strong. Strong breathing acts as a stimulus inside your body and quickly draws your consciousness inside, merging deep within. These breathing practices are very effective if you have a lot of distracting thoughts or need to calm down. Holding the breath can quickly empty the inner space of the brain.

Gentle: Lower Dantian Breathing, Qi Body Breathing, Universal Breathing, Lingjue Breathing, Tianmen Breathing — the air goes through the nose, mouth, lungs, all very slowly and gently. These types of breathing require relaxation and a focused consciousness state to create the entirety state.

If Distracting Thoughts Emerge

Distracting thoughts may still emerge during breathing practices. If the thoughts are strong enough to disrupt your meditation, try strong breathing methods like Throat Breathing or holding your breath for a while. This can mobilize the internal qi of your whole body, create a strong feeling, and clear any obstructions.

When distracting thoughts disappear, return again to the gentle breathing.

THROAT BREATHING

Key Points

Strengthens and mobilizes internal qi

Brings consciousness inside to observe subtle spaces

Why Throat Breathing?

This type of breathing is rougher and coarser than regular breathing. It has the potential to stabilize and focus your consciousness, induce calm, and draw qi into Lower Dantian to strengthen vitality and health.

Throat Breathing can readily:

- Activate and integrate your body's internal qi — through the qi of all the internal organs merging together

- Bring a lot of oxygen into the body

- Strengthen internal qi by drawing gentle pressure into the Middle Dantian and Lower Dantian

- Open areas of rougher, denser qi blockages

Variations: You can choose to practice Throat Breathing with stronger or gentler breaths, depending on how you feel. You can also practice Throat Breathing while sitting, standing, or lying down. It is common to feel "asleep but not asleep" with this practice.

Keep the upper and lower rows of teeth gently touching and pressing together. In the beginning, you can breathe through the mouth with the mouth slightly open — this can help you open the back of your throat. Once you know how to do Throat Breathing, breathe through your nose with the mouth closed.

Note: If you feel dizzy during this practice, it means the qi has influenced your brain. If you decrease the intensity, the qi in your cervical vertebrae will open and flow more freely. As the qi becomes more abundant in your body, the dizziness will disappear.

The Practice

Draw your mind into Shenji Palace (the center of your head). Soften the gaze.

Bring a gentle smile to your face, feeling your lips extend from ear to ear. Make your throat rounded, like there is a qi ball inside it.

Breathe in, keeping your throat open and rounded, as though the qi ball is expanding within.

Breathe out, keeping the throat open and rounded. Feel the coarse vibrations in your throat.

Continue this pattern, feeling the vibrations in your throat. Then expand the in-breath deep into the Middle Dantian (chest) and Lower Dantian (abdomen) — like balloons inflating in each cavity. The breathing is full. The entire inner space of the lung expands.

Do not focus, however, on the vibrations. Just observe whatever happens.

When you breathe out, make a rough sound with the exhaling air. Continue to feel the qi movement in the lungs, in the Middle and Lower Dantian spaces, and in the whole body — like a tiger!

You may feel the energy rise along both sides of your face (along the outer edges of the eyes), in your brain, and in Upper Dantian (center of the head). The throat remains open and expanded like a big qi channel.

This breathing goes from the Middle Channel down to the inner spaces of the Middle and Lower Dantian. Everything is connected through this breath. Upper, Middle, and Lower Dantian qi is all harmonized together as one.

Continue Throat Breathing, in, out… in, out….

Bring your awareness to the inner space of the Mingmen Inner Palace (anterior to the L2-L3 lumbar spine). Feel how the qi movement connects with the qi skin and how the surface of the skin is breathing. Every place in the body connects with Mingmen Inner Palace. It is the center of the breath.

You may also **hold your breath** for a short while. Breathe into Mingmen Inner Palace and hold your breath inside Mingmen. Relax as much as possible as you hold the breath.

When you feel that the internal qi is sufficiently activated and strengthened, and that the observer merges well with the internal qi, switch to Soft and Gentle Breathing.

When you are finished, hold a qi ball in front of Lower Dantian. Gently and slowly raise it up to above the head. Lower the hands toward Baihui, pouring qi down through the crown, Upper Dantian, Middle Dantian, and Lower Dantian. Place your hands on Duqi.

Rest there a while.

Soft and Gentle Breathing

Soft and Gentle Breathing starts from Shenji Palace. This practice gives the experience of the brain breathing, soft and gentle. And as the brain breathes, Shenji Palace expands to Tianmen (Heavenly Gate), which opens to and connects with the universe. This breathing connects Shenji Palace with the purest level of qi, or universal qi.

With the in-breath, the very pure, harmonious qi from the universe draws down through the Heavenly Gate to the brain. This universal qi nourishes the brain, making it very comfortable. The brain is a pure qi space, so it is very good and important to experience comfort there.

This pure qi experience expands down through the Middle Channel to Middle Dantian, Lower Dantian, Huiyin, and the rest of the body. With each breath, your awareness stays in Shenji Palace, Middle Dantian, Lower Dantian, and the Middle Channel. While your primary awareness is on these three centers, your peripheral awareness expands to the whole body. So the deep comfort in the brain space now expands and brings beautiful information to the whole body — the whole qi body is breathing.

In Soft and Gentle Breathing, you can also turn your awareness to the Mingmen Inner Palace as the center of this breathing. Consciousness focuses in Mingmen Inner Palace as you practice. It can become deeper and deeper; and perhaps activate Fetus Breathing (see Fetus Breathing below). Enjoy this "entirety breathing!"

The Practice

Draw your mind into Shenji Palace. Soften the gaze.

Breathe in and out, softly and gently. Feel the inner spaces of Shenji Palace, the Upper Dantian, and the brain — and connect them with the tip of your nose. In, out. In, out.

This is the movement of pure qi. Relax. Open more. Observe all the brain cells breathing. The Heavenly Gate (the top of the head) is open and breathing, too. When you breathe in, bring the universal qi down through the Heavenly Gate. Bring this qi through the Upper Dantian space, down through neck inner space, through the lungs, the Middle Dantian, through Hun Yuan Qiao, the Lower Dantian, the Mingmen Inner Palace, all the way down to Huiyin.

Feel the big qi column from the Heavenly Gate all the way down to Huiyin: this is a big qi space. This big qi column is called **the Middle Channel**. From the Middle Channel, the qi expands to fill the inner space of the arms, legs, and spine.

Repeat this sequence: observe qi flowing through your nose to the Upper Dantian. Draw universal qi down again through the Heavenly Gate, the Middle Channel, then the arms, legs, and spine. Relax the Upper Dantian, Middle Dantian, Lower Dantian.

Baihui at the crown of the head connects with Huiyin: gently lift up Huiyin. Qi from the universe goes down through the inner space down to Huiyin. Gradually, feel how qi along the Middle Channel merges with the whole body to fill all the internal space.

Feel the internal space of the whole body breathing with each of your breaths.

Do not think, "Breathe in and expand" or "Breathe out and expand." Just observe what happens internally. Observe this new level of reality. Now shift your focus to the surface of the qi body — the "qi skin" that covers your whole body. Observe your skin as a qi state. Feel that the skin is breathing.

Connect again with the qi space of the Middle Channel. Not with too much precision; just like a big qi column. Feel the qi skin of the whole body and observe deeper. Focus on the qi skin and experience how it is moving, breathing. This is the entire qi body breathing.

When you are finished, hold a qi ball in front of Lower Dantian. Gently and slowly raise it up to above the head. Lower the hands toward Baihui, pouring qi down through the crown, Upper Dantian, Middle Dantian, and Lower Dantian. Place your hands on Duqi. Rest there a while.

Fetus Breathing or Innate Breathing

The fetus in the mother's womb doesn't breathe with her nose, mouth, and lungs, but breathes with Lower Dantian qi. This practice can activate Fetus Breathing.

Why Fetus Breathing?

- When Fetus Breathing appears, your life force will be greatly enhanced.
- Many feel an increase in their inner happiness.
- Sexual energy can be activated, which can enhance overall health.

How to Practice

If you bring your observation into the Lower Dantian and Mingmen Inner Palace for a long time while doing Soft and Gentle Breathing, their qi spaces can become increasingly pure. And as all thoughts stop for increasingly longer stretches of time, your breathing may stop altogether. When this happens, Fetus Breathing is activated.

There is no thinking. No desire. No feelings. It is a state of total surrender.

Students generally feel the space of Lower Dantian becoming very harmonious and stable. If feelings or sexual energy emerge, do not attach to them. Just continue to surrender. The breathing is happening there, slightly and gently.

Lingjue Breathing or Mingjue Breathing

Lingjue is another word for Mingjue.

Ling means awakening or aware.

Jue means observation or observer.

Lingjue means the awakening observer.

When Mingjue merges with the breath, it is called Mingjue Breathing or Lingjue Breathing — they are the same thing.

With this breathing method, the feeling of the inhalation and exhalation goes directly into and out of Mingjue. It is as if Mingjue is breathing from the center of the head.

Mingjue also observes and reflects the breathing.

How to Practice

When you breathe in, notice the feeling on the tip of the nose. And from the tip of the nose, this feeling follows the nasal canal into the head and into the center of the brain.

Notice that when you breath in, there is a very light feeling happening in your brain. When you breathe out, just relax.

Close your eyes and look inside your head. Do you notice a feeling happening there? This breathing sensation is happening in the pure observer. And inside the observer, there is a knowing.

The key point is the feeling of the breath that happens in the pure observer, and at the same time, the observer observes itself breathing — it happens within the clear mirror. When the observer knows itself, Mingjue appears.

Even though the feeling happens in the head, the focus is not on the feeling, but on the knowing — knowing that it is Mingjue who knows.

This sensory experience of breathing helps you realize that you are the observer. When Mingjue appears, the breathing happens continuously in the pure Mingjue state. Mingjue is always present.

The breathing sensation inside your head gradually expands, going down through the neck and chest, the Middle Dantian and Lower Dantian. Mingjue also appears in these spaces.

Once you have the basics of this breathing down, you can realize that Mingjue is breathing in universal qi from the galaxy. (It actually comes into the center of the head through the Heavenly Gate on top of the head).

Two Primary Points

- Focus on Mingjue during the breathing
- Receive the information from the pure universal qi field, trusting that it makes Mingjue more powerful and clear as well as nourishes the body

The Practice

Relax your gaze. Relax the entire body. Now relax your breath.

When you breathe in, notice the very slight feeling on the tip of the nose. From there, follow it to the center of your head.

Completely relax the brain so the feeling in your brain is very comfortable. Be aware that the observer is aware of the feeling. Through this feeling, the observer becomes clear to itself: this is Mingjue. And the feeling is in Mingjue.

Your breathing remains very gentle. The breath, from the tip of the nose to the inner head, merges with Mingjue. Each time the feeling of breathing happens, feel Mingjue clearly.

Breathe in, breathe out. Feel how the sensation extends through the neck and chest. Mingjue is also in the neck and chest.

The breathing sensation goes down to Middle Dantian and Lower Dantian. Mingjue is also in these spaces. The feeling of the breath is always in Mingjue.

Relax more. Follow the breathing sensations and realize that Mingjue goes throughout the whole body. Feel the breathing. This pure feeling is also in the entire Mingjue space within the body.

The body becomes very harmonious. Observe how the breathing intensifies Mingjue.

Practice this for 20-30 minutes if you can.

When you are finished, hold a qi ball in front of Lower Dantian. Slowly raise the qi ball to above the head. Pour qi down through Baihui, the neck, chest, and abdomen. Place hands on Duqi.

Rest there for a while.

Variation: When you exhale, say ṅ (see Repeating the ṅ Sound in the subsequent section, Sound Practices). So when you breathe in, the feeling and Mingjue are one. When you breathe out, ṅ and Mingjue are one.

Universe Breathing

Key Points

- Observation: draw consciousness inside, deeper and deeper
- Qi body breathing –> qi field breathing –> universe breathing

How to Practice

When we practice Universe Breathing, the first step is to observe and to feel the inner space of the body.

You are universal qi. If you observe yourself with physical eyes, you may experience yourself as the physical body. But if you close your eyes and just use your consciousness to observe the qi body — because the body is empty space — you can feel that you are qi, and you and the galaxy are one.

Universe Breathing should start with strong breathing, like Throat Breathing (covered earlier in this section), which makes the internal qi of the body merge together. This deepens your observation and concentration.

The Qi Body Breathing gradually expands to become Qi Field Breathing, going beyond the boundaries of the body — this means that when you breathe, the whole qi field breathes with you. Observe the pure universal space and feel the universe breathing, step by step.

Gradually, your can make your breathing gentler and gentler.

The Notable Pause

Observe and feel the pause between the in-breath and the out-breath — a momentary but important gap. For some, this pause is shorter, for others longer. You need not feel the pause. Just be aware that it is there.

This pause is the key to open the entire time-space. This means that, in the pause, you can lose your sense of time and space, going beyond these dimensions into "no time" and "no space."

This pause, therefore, brings you from observing yourself as qi to knowing yourself as consciousness. The very pure quality of qi is already close to consciousness. When you observe the pause, the observation of consciousness will naturally happen. Just observe and experience. Then you will come to know the state of your consciousness — how the observer feels.

Do not overthink this! When you think or ask how, then you may never experience it. Just do it.

The Practice

Note: This practice can be done saying Shenji or ñ. To improve Mingjue, the primary practice is to say ñ.

Sit straight with a comfortable posture. Relax the whole body.

Draw consciousness into Shenji Palace. Relax and draw your gaze inward, and observe Shenji Palace. Feel deep within Shenji Palace. By observing deeper into Shenji Palace, you can gradually come to experience inner peace.

Observe Shenji Palace and say ñ.

With an inner smile, silently say ñ. Notice and feel the brain immediately relaxing.

Shenji Palace becomes more open. ñ… ñ… ñ….

With an inner smile, gradually say ñ faster and faster, staying relaxed. Then faster yet, but silently. With training, this will become easier to do in a relaxed state. Notice how, when you say ñ faster, you become more focused. When you observe any distracting thoughts, you can say ñ very fast.

Now slow down and relax. Feel consciousness focused — feel your consciousness becoming independent, a kind of invisible, independent power.

Clearly observe the internal space of the brain. Observe the space of Upper Dantian opening to the universe. In your consciousness, truly realize the infinite emptiness of universe: it is a pure qi state.

Feel the infinite universe. The emptiness in your consciousness is the universal qi state. Do not use your nervous system and five senses to measure the infinite universe. Just use your consciousness to go throughout the universe and know the universal space. Realize that the space is not completely empty — it is made up of pure qi. Your consciousness is also pure qi, and it expands to fill up the universe.

Feel this emptiness connect with the emptiness inside your body. When you observe inside the body, you realize that it, too, has the emptiness of the universe. The inner space of the body, however, also has sensations that move through the nervous system. The nervous system is also qi. Your consciousness can observe and feel inside the body. The pure qi of the empty, infinite universe merges with the space of the qi body.

In the infinite universal space, your consciousness merges together with the field of the whole World Consciousness Community. Feel this collective consciousness field becoming stronger. With your heart open to the collective field and to the qi universe, feel it relaxed and very light: the heart is free.

The whole world consciousness field now observes the inner space of your head and observes:

> The inner space of the neck. Empty….

> The inner space of the shoulders, arms, Middle Dantian, and Lower Dantian. Empty….

> The inner space of the spine. Empty….

> The inner space of the legs. Empty….

> The whole body's inner space. Empty….

Relax… open… merge into the infinite universe. At the same time, the universal pure qi comes into the body and penetrates deep within. Feel the pure emptiness permeate throughout the body, into the deep inner space of all the cells. The experience in consciousness is of pure emptiness and of pure universal qi. This very pure qi is empty.

Relax... open....

Gently use Throat Breathing to integrate the qi of the universe and the internal qi of the body. Use the power of bodily qi to draw in universal pure qi and transform universal pure qi within the body. Maintain this universal pure qi within the body. Throat Breathing goes through Upper Dantian, Middle Dantian and Lower Dantian. Observe the throat's strong, rough feeling, and experience the very pure, empty space within the rough feeling — this is universal qi. Go into the rough feeling, which comes from the nervous system, but do not be limited by it. Go beyond it.

Now use Soft and Gentle Breathing and relax your breathing. Notice how the rough feeling decreases, then disappears. Feel how the inner space and the infinite universe have now become one. The limitation of the rough feeling has disappeared, and the pure emptiness of the universe appears in the body's internal space. When you focus on this very pure experience, the limitations of the body will disappear.

There is still a very subtle feeling — this feeling connects the inner space with the universal pure qi, far, far away.

Relax more. The more relaxed you are, the more you will be aware of the purer levels. Allow your breathing to become very light. This is Universe Breathing.

When you come to this very pure level, observe and experience how this fine universal qi enters and permeates the qi body. The inner space of the body nearly disappears as it becomes universal space. You and the universe have become one.

Observe that the infinite emptiness has no boundaries — only infinite depth.

Observe the infinite emptiness. Observe a very gentle, slight pure qi movement in the infinite emptiness. This is the Universe Breathing.

In this breathing, observe the in-breath and then a pause. Then the out-breath and then a pause. The pause it is very even, very pure.

The secret is in the pause: Observe the pause clearly between each inhalation and exhalation. This is the portal that opens you beyond the entire time-space structure, meaning you step outside of time and space. No time exists: you just are. No space exists: you are everywhere.

Stay relaxed. Continuously observe Universe Breathing.

When you are ready, come into Throat Breathing again. Observe deep inside this rougher feeling. Come fully back to the form of your physical body. Move your feet, legs, hands, and arms slowly.

When you are finished, hold a qi ball in front of Lower Dantian. Gently and slowly raise it up to above the head. Lower the hands toward Baihui, pouring qi down through the crown, Upper Dantian, Middle Dantian, and Lower Dantian. Place your hands on Duqi.

Rest there a while.

SOUND PRACTICES OVERVIEW

In Zhineng Qigong, sounds are used to:

- Develop observation and concentration
- Mobilize qi
- Transform emotional energy at the organ level
- Heal yourself and others

SEVEN TYPES OF SOUND EXPERIENCE

1. Feeling the vibration — loud sounds are strong and rough. Silent sounds have very fine and subtle vibrations.

2. Observing the sounds — what you notice is not the vibrations, but the sounds. You can hear the sounds in your consciousness.

3. Observing the thoughts — thoughts of the sounds precede you making the sounds.

4. Observing the information — the information of the sounds precedes the thoughts; it is already in your consciousness.

5. Observing the intention — there is an intention to think of a sound and also an intention to observe it. The intention to say and observe it comes before the thought, and comes before the information that is already in consciousness. Can you feel it very deeply? If there is no intention, you will not be able to experience this level. The information forms the intention, and the information of the intention further activates information.

6. Observing the emptiness — the intention happens from and within the emptiness. Sounds, thoughts, and information all happen in the emptiness. Who is observing the vibrations, sounds, thoughts, information, intention and emptiness?

7. The observer coming to itself: Mingjue appearing — Mingjue is an awakening state of emptiness. It is empty, but it is an awakening emptiness.

FOUR LEVELS OF SOUND

1. Audible sounds — loud, soft, fast, slow, short, long

During intense life experiences, you can repeat sounds loudly and rapidly to purify Mingjue, qi, and the body — to bring you directly into Mingjue state, into the present moment, connected to self.

2. Silent sounds — internal sounds, tongue, air movement

3. Thinking the sounds — "hearing the sounds" in thought

4. Feeling the intention of the sounds without thinking or saying them ("think but not think," "do not think but think") — simply holding an awareness of the sounds but not actively thinking about them. This level is also called "mind sound" or "thought sound."

Focus on observing the sounds, vibrations, and also observing your thoughts. Then you may not get so easily attached to the vibratory sensations or the experience of the sounds.

"I am observing Mingjue initiating the sounds." Then the sounds become Mingjue — they merge.

REPEATING SHENJI

Key Points

Observe: Shenji Palace in the center of the head

Relax: inner smile, Shenji Palace turns into empty space

Concentrate: focus deeper into ever smaller qi spaces

Repeating Shenji is a tool to help you realize that you are the observer, and that you are observing the sound Shenji.

Since the function of the observer is to observe, Shenji is the object, or the information that the observer observes.

What is Shenji Palace?

Shenji Palace is an extremely important space in Zhineng Qigong: it is the palace of consciousness. This area is ripe with potential — many "super abilities," like intuition and extrasensory perceptions, can be developed from this place.

At the Huaxia Center ("Medicineless Hospital in China"), Dr. Pang taught that an extended practice of Repeating Shenji would greatly develop the potential of consciousness.

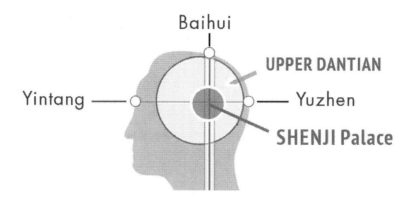

Where is Shenji Palace?

Shenji Palace is in the center of the head. This area can be said to be the "third eye." Many have believed that the third eye is between the eyebrows, but it is actually found in the pineal gland area. In the practice of Repeating Shenji, you need to know the location of Shenji Palace. Study the diagram above.

More specifically, Shenji Palace is the space where two lines cross each other: if you draw an imaginary horizontal line from Yingtang between the eyebrows to Yuzhen at the back of the head (a small protrusion at the base of the skull), and another imaginary line vertically downward from Baihui, Shenji Palace is where they cross.

Repeating the sound Shenji will activate a specific vibration in Shenji Palace.

SHENJI PALACE AND SUPER ABILITIES

Two different kinds of super abilities can be developed, related to directionality:

1. **Going forward** — if you move consciousness or qi forward (horizontally) from Shenji Palace, you can open the third eye's function and develop the super ability of "seeing through." This means you can gain the ability to:

- See through someone else's body. His or her body becomes transparent.

- See through to the level that you want to see and even diagnose a problem.

- See the different layers of the body and even see colors at different levels.

2. **Going upward** — when you move consciousness or qi upward (vertically) from Shenji Palace to the Heavenly Gate, you can develop another, more fundamental, super ability: direct knowledge or intuition.

This means you can:

- Gain access to knowledge or information — direct intuition
- Know things happening in a different time or place

Awakening Shenji Palace

Repeating Shenji unleashes the vibration of Shenji Palace. When you focus on this vibration, your consciousness will come back from the external world and remain centered in this place. This is likened to a master staying in his or her palace. When your consciousness remains in Shenji Palace, you can be the master of your life.

Shenji Palace is an exceptionally good place to train your focus and concentration.

The Sound Shenji Carries Double Information

There are two Chinese characters to this sound, and each gathers and carries a lot of cultural information. When you say shen 神 the vibration happens inside Shenji Palace. When you say ji 机, qi gathers in the center of Shenji Palace.

- When you practice Repeating Shenji, you must combine concentration and relaxation. If you just concentrate and your focus is too strong, you can create tension in the center of the head. So relax the sounds — and relax the intention. Shenji Palace is a pure, relaxed space.

- Repeating Shenji naturally helps you focus inward, so distracting thoughts interfere less with your practice.

Relaxation Can Happen in Two Ways

- You relax your intention and focus with a little inner smile.

- At the same time, you relax inwardly.

If you have a lot of mental distractions: practice saying Shenji more rapidly — either strongly or gently. Either way, the vibration draws your focus of consciousness into Shenji Palace and distracting thoughts vanish. Even if some thoughts appear, active thinking generally subsides.

REPEATING SHENJI HEALS TRAUMA

Shen Ji

You can send information through the gentle vibrations of Repeating Shenji. This simple sound can open up old, fixed mental and emotional patterns that block or slow down the flow of qi.

With past traumatic experiences, strong emotional memories can create strong qi blockages in the brain and become imprinted in the mind. These memories can then create qi blockages and express as physical symptoms. Remembering a trauma elicits an immediate reaction in both the body and the mind. This memory can materialize as health challenges.

With regular practice of Repeating Shenji, the inner space of the brain can readily harmonize and flow, merging more readily with universal space or qi. When you say Shenji, all thoughts vanish, so it is difficult to recall past events. The internal space just feels empty and this emptiness feels harmonious. Over time, the old, fixed reference framework loses its strength and power. Only the experience of qi and emptiness remains.

Tip 1: When you say Shenji, keep your intention and sounds relaxed. Keep a gentle inner smile. Sometimes people can feel tension in Shenji Palace if they say Shenji for too long a period. If this happens, draw your consciousness down to the Mingmen Inner Palace (anterior to the L2-L3 lumbar spine) and say Shenji within that space. The tension inside Shenji Palace will disappear.

Tip 2: In some books, they talk about a "background." This can cause confusion and create a conceptual separation. So Teacher Wei recommends this:

After you are in the Mingjue state and continue to say Shenji, simply feel that the sound Shenji is the movement of Mingjue, that Mingjue is using the information of "shen" and "ji," choosing this information and reflecting it. The function and the being of Mingjue are one. The pause between the sounds is also Mingjue. There is no background. Mingjue occupies the whole time-space dimension.

The Practice

For beginners: Start by practicing Repeating Shenji in the Mingjue state for just 15 to 20 minutes. This may avoid possible heaviness or discomfort in the head. Gradually, you can practice longer and longer.

For more advanced students: Can you practice Repeating Shenji alone for one to two hours?

Sit up straight, gently lifting up the Baihui at the crown of the head, feet planted on the floor. Soften your gaze.

From the place between the eyebrows, draw your consciousness directly into the center of the head to Shenji Palace. Focus into Shenji Palace and feel that space.

Say Shenji softly. When you say shen, observe the vibration in Shenji Palace. When you say ji, observe qi drawing into Shenji Palace.

Use soft sounds to repeat Shenji... Shenji... Shenji.... Give a gentle inner smile and relax inwardly. Focus in the center of your head and also relax your intention.

Repeat Shenji... Shenji... Shenji.... Feel Shenji palace open its internal space, becoming more open. Continue observing and focusing in the center. The greater the feeling of internal openness, the greater the feeling of internal lightness and emptiness. Repeat Shenji...Shenji...Shenji.... When the vibrations of Shenji become very clear, whisper Shenji so others cannot hear your sounds, but continue the movement of the mouth and tongue and the flow of air. Feel the vibrations in Shenji Palace becoming subtler, finer. Observe the finer vibrations. And relax.

Continue to whisper Shenji... Shenji... Shenji.... Observe the internal space of Shenji Palace as a very small space, like the tip of a needle. Observe deeper, staying relaxed. When you feel Shenji Palace becoming so peaceful that you fall silent, at that point, just think Shenji within Shenji Palace. Observe the gentle, slight vibration there becoming finer and finer. If you cannot feel the vibration, still continue saying Shenji silently.

Continue to repeat silently and observe what is happening inside Shenji Palace — to the brain, brain cells, and blood vessels. Observe what happens in that space, what happens in the entire inner space of the head — the pure vibration from Shenji Palace spreading throughout the head. This vibration penetrates the brain's nerve cells, which become a more harmonious qi entirely. Observe the left brain and right brain merging together. Small internal blockages transform and disappear. Send good information deep inside Shenji Palace to change any past difficult (blocked) patterns and memories. Only qi remains.

Relax more with an inner smile. The vibration of Shenji merges with universal space.

Now just think Shenji... Shenji... Shenji.... You can go to a deeper level by observing the thought shen and the thought ji and then go beyond the thought. Notice that the vibration is still there, then go beyond the vibration. Notice how you just changed your focus on the thoughts. Experience the state of the moment just before the thought happens.

As the thought is about to appear — but before it does — notice that you have an intention, a motivation. Actually, there are a lot of movements happening. Information gathers, but you do not need to mind this. Just feel how, before the thought appears, there is an internal, very subtle intention. When you observe the intention, realize that your focus is not on the thoughts. This is a kind of highly focused state.

Now realize who is observing the information of shen and ji. Who is observing the information?

At this moment, you are observing the observer. And the information of shen and ji is appearing inside the observer. The observer is like a pure, invisible mirror, and the double information (shen and ji) is very clearly reflected in the mirror. Because the information appears in the mirror, this proves there is a mirror. Focus on the mirror, not the information. The mirror has the function to reflect the information.

Continue to silently repeat the two sounds, being fully aware of their two-fold information. Relax as much as possible. Observation, concentration, and relaxation are all working together.

Shenji… Shenji… Shenji….

If your Mingjue state is very pure and the experience of observing the observer is very deep, your intention may disappear. When the intention disappears, you are just pure Mingjue — you are in a state of Being.

When you are ready to finish the practice, draw your consciousness down to Mingmen Inner Palace. Relax the head while consciousness stays in Mingmen Inner Palace — sleep there for a while and merge with the innate pure qi of that space. When Mingjue comes down, qi also comes down.

Relax a while. Feel Mingmen breathing. The breathing is also in Mingjue, and is reflected in the pure mirror. The inner space of the head becomes lighter and lighter. Notice how any tension disappears.

Just stay there, relaxed inside Mingmen's inner space.

When you are ready, slowly restore your vision, continuously thinking Shenji inwardly — and throughout your day.

Homework

1. In addition to practicing the above meditation, try thinking Shenji very fast, but very relaxed. In one minute, think Shenji 100 times. Just use the information: "In one minute, I can think Shenji a hundred times," and trust that you can do this. Do not question it. Just relax and do it. Do this so fast that you cannot even feel that you are thinking the words shen and ji one at a time.

2. Going further: Work your way up to thinking Shenji ten thousand times in one second, or even millions of times in one second. "Thinking Shenji one million times a second" means that you cannot count the number of times it is repeated because you are not falling into that linear habit. Rather, you are just trusting your great potential — the potential for super abilities — because this information works in Yiyuanti. All you need is to have this information, and in that state, your consciousness will work very, very fast, even faster than the Internet.

REPEATING THE ṅ SOUND

To enter the Mingjue state and eventually come to Yiyuanti (or True Self), there are many tools. Repeating Shenji is one. Another is repeating the simple sound ṅ. Since 2010, Dr. Pang taught the practice Repeating the ṅ Sound and found it to be **the most effective way to develop Mingjue**.

Repeating ṅ is different than the practice of Repeating Shenji, in that it is a single sound, a single letter, and there is no meaning. There is no Chinese character for this sound. It is a very simple kind of information — at the level of essence. So when you say ṅ the vibration is a movement of invisible qi.

If you just think ṅ, this is very, very pure information. While words can carry energy because they carry meaning, the ṅ sound, without any meaning, does not carry energy. **It is pure information**.

Dr. Pang said ṅ conveys the true state of Yiyuanti. This means that the Yiyuanti state can manifest in the ṅ sound. ṅ is nothing, but it is also something: it is ṅ.

When we say ṅ it is very simple and pure and directly reveals Yiyuanti. It comes to Yiyuanti and awakens Yiyuanti to itself.

Repeating the ṅ Sound Helps Mingjue "Grow Up"

• **Cultivating independence and confidence** — when you practice the ṅ sound, you can gradually experience your Mingjue as independent and confident. Be mindful that this independence is not in conflict with anything else; it is a very harmonious entirety state. This independent consciousness holds everything and merges with everything. The confidence of Mingjue is unconditional, as well as safe and stable. There is no need to compare it to anything else. Just trust its presence and confidence.

• **Experiencing Mingjue deeper and longer** — you can say ṅ inside your body in any internal space, or in the whole Qi Entirety, even in the whole qi universe. When the pure Mingjue simply says ṅ in one space, that space will become harmonized and purified. Mingjue can use ñ to transform qi at a deeper level.

Saying ñ Sound in Daily Life

Repeating the ñ Sound can readily bring you to the present moment and into a pure, clear, and peaceful Mingjue state. So if you always say ñ in your daily life, you can gradually increase the amount of time you stay in this state.

For example, when you feel that you are fixating on something, you can suddenly think or say ñ… and come back to yourself. Repeating the ñ Sound… "Oh, I lost myself! ñ… ñ… ñ… ñ…!" Come back! ñ… returns Mingjue toward your True Self. ñ… I am here! Not on the watermelon, not on that person, not an event external to me.

You can connect with that something or someone, but ñ reminds you to stay here, stay clearly in the present moment. Gradually, you will ground inside yourself, ground and root in your Mingjue, and also connect to the world to form an entirety. If you have no roots, your fears and worries increase and you will want to look for something external to yourself for support — it's akin to being homeless. When you root inside your inner observer, you can come to experience, "Oh, my home is here, I am at home." ñ… ñ… ñ….

Walking Meditation

Repeat the ñ sound as you walk. Walk around your house, saying ñ…. Or walk around your neighborhood or in a park. You can also think or silently say ñ….

Even when you talk with others, your consciousness can still hold ñ there. You can speak with your mouth, but your Pure Consciousness can think ñ at the same time.

Gradually, ñ becomes a state in your Pure Consciousness.

Running Meditation

If you enjoy running, practice ñ while running. When you are running, the qi of your whole body is flowing well.

What Not to Do

Refrain from asking questions like, "When will I become enlightened?" or, "When will I come to True Self?"

Repeating the ñ Sound is a **practice in surrender.** You must learn to surrender your questions, surrender your thoughts, totally relax your body, open your heart, and surrender to the entirety. With surrender, we cannot think our way into this state; that is, do not think, "I need to surrender," "I need to accept everything." Just practice! Practice total surrender and acceptance in the Mingjue state.

How to Practice

When you are just learning how to practice ň, it may be easier to keep the lips and front teeth slightly open. Relax the tongue, keeping it almost flat. The middle and the back parts of the tongue will have very little movement. Inside the mouth, keep an empty space.

When you become more skilled, you do not need to open your mouth. Make the ň sound with a closed mouth — it is an internal sound.

Say ň. From the middle of the tongue (slightly behind the middle), feel how there is a vibration that connects with the inner space of the head. If you observe the inner space of the head, you can feel the sound and vibration surging upward — toward and through the Shenji Palace to the top of the head.

In the beginning, practice saying ň more loudly. This can help clear distracting thoughts and bring your full attention to ň. Over time, you can soften it and also say ň silently. You can experience the vibrations of ň anywhere in the body, wherever you focus your consciousness.

Do not use any force. Do not hold any tension. Totally relax. If you think too much, you cannot practice ň well.

Keep it Simple!

Dr. Pang taught this from the outset: ň is very simple; there is only one letter. If you judge or think too much — whether it's the movement, tongue, teeth, mouth — you will lose the meaning of ň. The simple sound is important, but the state when you say ň is more important. Do not become entangled in the details — this risks putting too much information on ň and complicating ň. Simple is better!

ň... is a direct way to practice Yiyuanti. To practice ň doesn't mean you have achieved the Yiyuanti (enlightenment) level, or even that you have experienced the Yiyuanti state. ň... is a function of Yiyuanti and is therefore a way that Yiyuanti receives information. Exercising the functions of Yiyuanti allows you to awaken to Yiyuanti.

ñ is an Unbroken Sound

When you practice ñ, you are repeating the ñ sound, unbroken. There is a pause between the sounds, but Mingjue connects each ñ sound to the one before and after it, connected in the flow of time and space by the empty pause in between — like an unbroken chain. If you say ñ and then get distracted with other thoughts, then the chain is broken.

Practice ñ as an unbroken, continuous sound. When you can experience this, this means an improving Mingjue Gongfu practice.

The empty space is also ñ

Be aware of the empty space between each ñ sound. Mingjue is in the emptiness, too.

Who knows ñ?

The most important thing in this practice is to ask yourself, "Where does ñ come from?" "Where does ñ appear? Then just focus on ñ, observe ñ, and observe the information happening inside the observer.

When you are starting this practice, you can say or think that ñ is reflected within Mingjue. Over time, you will feel that ñ is Mingjue, Mingjue is ñ. The observer and ñ become one.

Always ask yourself:

> Who knows ñ?
> Who says ñ?
> Who observes ñ?

The Practice

Sit up straight, gently lifting Baihui up toward the sky, your feet on the ground. Relax your gaze. Relax the whole body.

Bring consciousness back to the center of the head. Observe Pure Consciousness. Relax Shenji Palace. Relax the brain. Relax the Upper Dantian space. Relax the neck. Relax the shoulders and arms. Relax the chest, abdomen, spine, and legs.

Observe the whole qi body.

Pure Consciousness merges with the whole qi body and observes within to a very subtle level. Be relaxed, be peaceful.

Now say ñ… ñ… ñ…. Feel Mingjue saying ñ… ñ… ñ…. Feel the entirety saying ñ. It is the pure clear observer who says ñ. Mingjue says ñ…. ñ is in Mingjue.

Observe the ñ sound. ñ… appears clearly in your consciousness. ñ… ñ… ñ…. (Repeat this many times.)

Relax. Sleep but not sleep.

Do not focus on the feeling or the vibration — simply observe ñ and observe Mingjue saying ñ. ñ happens in pure Mingjue, making Mingjue clearer, stabler, simpler. When you say ñ, the ñ sound and Mingjue are one. There is nothing else.

Continue saying ñ… ñ… ñ…. Stay in the ñ state with an inner smile. Be aware of each ñ sound clearly. Be aware of the empty space between each ñ sound. Observe each ñ sound as connected to all the other ñ sounds in a continuous, unbroken chain, connected by the emptiness in between, all in the flow of time and space. Mingjue is in the emptiness, too.

Say ñ… ñ… ñ….

Mingjue goes throughout the whole qi body, observing ñ wherever it focuses: (scanning slowly) the Upper Dantian space, neck inner space, Middle Dantian, Lower Dantian, the inner space of the spine. Do not mind any other sensations besides ñ. Mingjue goes into the shoulders and arms, then the legs and feet. Relax.

Mingjue remains very pure and peaceful and merges with the whole qi body. Breathe into Mingmen, focus on Mingmen, bring qi down into Mingmen Inner Palace.

Hold a qi ball and lift qi up, slowly to above the head, pour qi down, through the Upper Dantian, the neck, Middle Dantian, Lower Dantian. Then place palms on Duqi.

Stay inside the ñ state — as if your consciousness is still saying ñ. Observe your peaceful inner state.

Separate hands to the side. Slowly restore your gaze.

(After restoring your gaze, remain in the clear Mingjue state and continuously say ñ… in your mind. This is how you can train Mingjue during your daily life.)

Suggestions for Daily Practice

Practice ñ daily for at least 30 minutes.

Practice going deeper, to a very pure and stable state where each ñ is perceived clearly in the Mingjue state and Mingjue is clearly in each ñ.

Sometimes you may practice ñ for one or two hours and feel like it was but an instant. This means you have come into the entire time-space state, where time and space disappear. This is the *ding* or *ru-ding state*.

If Thoughts Keep Coming

When Repeating the ñ Sound brings you to a pure Mingjue state, information from the universe can still appear and trigger your consciousness. That is, if Mingjue receives this information and links with the old information system or reference framework (which is in Mingjue), Mingjue can lose itself by following the thoughts.

When this happens, the best response is to continuously say or think ñ — faster and louder until consciousness becomes clear and focused again. This simple, single piece of information with no meaning occupies your Mingjue space. So if other information appears, it means the information of ñ is still weak and has not yet linked with the reference framework.

With continual practice, ñ will merge with Mingjue and go beyond all other information and thoughts. Other thoughts cannot happen; or if they do, ñ can quickly replace this other information.

The State of "Do Nothing"

Sometimes when you practice Mingjue, you will arrive at the state of "**do nothing**." This is also called the ***ru-ding state***, in which you have no thoughts or images. You are just the mirror reflecting everything. In this state, one or two hours can feel like an instant. This is because this state goes beyond the entire time-space structure, where linear time and space disappear. If you can stay in the Mingjue state of *ru-ding* for a day, or two, or three, your whole experience of life can become new.

Note: *Ru-ding* is simply a state where consciousness does nothing. Sometimes it is a Mingjue state, other times it is not. Do not judge. Just continue to observe without intention.

Asentando tu polvo interior: Try to find a few days during which you can totally simplify your life. Practice staying in the Mingjue state and try to limit conversations and screen time. Do only very simple activities like walking or eating, all in the Mingjue state. Remain quiet for a few days. This time and space can allow your inner space to calm down. Your inner state is like dust: when you remain quiet, the dust settles and the space becomes very clean and clear. Then your whole information system (or reference framework) can naturally reorganize and harmonize.

HEALING WITH ñ SOUND

ñ… can be used for healing.

After you come to the state where Mingjue and ñ have already become one, you can put healing information within ñ. For example, if you feel pain in your stomach, you can direct Mingjue there, and Mingjue says ñ in that space. ñ and Mingjue become one, so while you're practicing Mingjue in the space of the stomach, you're also sending it healing information with ñ because of your intention to heal that space.

Healing and Mingjue Practice Reinforce Each Other

Saying ñ into a challenged area can heal that area. But if you take it a step further and connect to who is doing the healing, asking "Who am I through this healing?" and then coming to know who you are, you might even become enlightened.

So this healing practice is also Mingjue Gongfu. Through healing practices, you continue to observe and experience how Mingjue sends information. This draws you deeper and deeper into Mingjue awareness.

Important: Keep your focus on the source of the information, not on the health condition, result, or body.

Healing Others with ñ

Find someone who needs healing. Carry the intention, focused but light, and connect to that person.

Come to your best and purest Mingjue state. Feel deep in your Mingjue state that there is the single information — ñ — and send this information to the person. As reviewed in Part 1: Theory, sending information is a function of Mingjue and Yiyuanti. Through sending information, Yiyuanti can suddenly realize itself: "Oh, I am sending information!"

Once you understand this, offer more healings for others. Do not become attached to the patient, the problems, the result, or even the function of Yiyuanti. Just experience and observe how Mingjue is sending information — that is, observe who is sending. Through this function of Yiyuanti, you can go directly to the pure source. This information is a kind of Mingjue or Yiyuanti "super ability."

Repeating the Sound Xü

In traditional practices in China, xü is a very important word — its information links the form and formless dimensions. When you say xü the qi becomes pure enough to merge with the source of universe: the Original Hun Yuan Qi.

When the observer observes itself — as you come to your True Self — it is also the xü state.

Xü is Both an Adjective and a Verb

Adjective: "empty but not empty," or the quality of the qi or consciousness state

Verb: 1- transforms form/matter into qi

    2- purifies qi and makes it finer and finer

    3- purifies consciousness more and more

Pronunciation: Xü can be difficult for non-Mandarin speakers to learn, but with repetition, anyone can learn to say it. Some language coaches describe the opening (sh) sound as being between a hiss and a whistle, with the lips puckered. The sound is best learned by repetitive listening and practice.

How to Practice

Close your eyes and observe the head's inner space. Then say xü. Feel how the perception of your head changes into formless qi.

Xü

You can say xü in the inner spaces of the body. In each small area, observe how the form of the body transforms into qi, and how the qi becomes finer and finer. As qi becomes increasingly finer, your qi body becomes increasingly finer, too.

Say xü, combining the sound and information in your consciousness. Create a very fine-tuned experience. The information of xü in your consciousness guides it to observe finer and finer levels.

Xü is its own intention — the information of the sound already contains the intention in your consciousness. When you practice Mingjue consciousness, saying xü is the same as thinking xü. The information will guide Mingjue. The awakening consciousness will become purer and purer, improving to a higher level. Mingjue observes all three levels of transformation at the same time.

If you have the time and awareness, you can practice xü for an entire day!

Reflection Question

Who is experiencing and observing the emptiness during this practice?

REPEATING HAOLA

Haola is a simple word/sound that means "All is well!"

The Haola Practice can be used to:

- Send someone good information (Example: after someone shares in a group)

- Enhance any movement practice (Example: repeating Haola! during Chen Qi)

- Bring healing to yourself or someone else (Example: repeating Haola! during a healing session)

It is very important to know and embody this word. Saying or writing haola is not enough. You must repeat it until you yourself **are the haola**, feeling it completely and always.

Important: When you give the information of haola, do this with the intention to improve consciousness and develop universal love and compassion. The information of haola is part of the Mingjue Entirety field. If you can truly realize this, the practice of Repeating Haola will contain deep power and meaning.

Conversely, if there is no understanding of haola — that is, if there is no sense of its importance and power for both personal and collective consciousness — this practice can become rote very quickly.

Therefore, simply saying haola to try to heal a patient is not enough. The patient also needs to feel that everything is haola. This is the entirety of healing — **a resonance of internal consciousness fields**. Do not focus on the outcome of your endeavor, because there is no endeavor. You just are. You just are love, light, beauty, kindness, compassion, and peace.

With the deeper consciousness dimension, the practice of Repeating Haola can benefit everyone and anyone. Even if the group cannot heal someone's health challenge, or perhaps the condition even worsens, you can still continue Repeating Haola and sending universal love. This is the deeper and larger practice — one that goes beyond results and outcomes.

Hao La

If You Don't Feel the Haola Spirit

You may not always feel the haola spirit. The information of haola, however, is your true nature. You can become more fully who you already are by letting go of things that are not in alignment with your True Self. Focusing on this one essence is enough. So you can relax. The healing will take care of itself.

Sometimes the lack of spirit is because your experience of haola is too narrow. For example, if you are focused on one person's benefit or that of a few people, and the focus is on a specific outcome, then limitations are most certain to arise. If the other person cannot be healed or if the person dies, you can feel grief, disappointment, fear, and doubt.

If you practice repeating the haola sound anyhow, over time, you will come to realize that these beautiful haola thoughts are revealing your inner beauty as well as the beautiful consciousness field, no matter what the outcome may be.

FOUNDATIONAL MINGJUE GONGFU PRACTICES

Open and Close, Kai He or La Qi

Key Points

- Observation, relaxation, concentration

- Penetration, expansion, merging and transforming (hunhua)

In Zhineng Qigong Theory, there are seven movements in the qi universe. Open and Close is the most fundamental movement.

Tian ren he yi means "humans and the universe are one." This state can be directly experienced by practicing the Qi Entirety (everything is qi). **Open and Close is one of the practices that can readily bring us to an experience of merging with the universe.**

When Mingjue observes the whole body as qi, then the whole universe as qi, there is no boundary between you and the entire qi universe. With no form, the qi body readily merges with universal qi, like a drop of water merging into the ocean. You become the universe. You connect to infinite power. Mingjue is infinite.

Tian Ren He Yi

How to Practice

The qi body does Open and Close — in qigong practice, the movements help the inner qi of the body completely open and close. Each organ and each cell are like this. In this open and flowing state, the body can become healthy.

Consciousness also does Open and Close — in Mingjue Gongfu practice, consciousness also trains through Open and Close — by practicing observation, relaxation, and concentration. The practice of Open and Close, therefore, becomes a movement of consciousness.

When you do Open and Close, it's important to know the purpose or intention — it is for transformation. This goes beyond observation.

The Basic Form

In the beginning, the practice of Open and Close focuses on the space between the hands and palms, as they hold a qi ball.

Hold your arms in front of Duqi, as if hugging a qi ball. Then cup your palms, your fingers slightly spread out like they are holding a small qi ball, gently, not too tight. Relax the arms, hands, and fingers.

Use your elbows to lead your arms and hands to slowly open and close. Your fingertips are facing each other — as if the fingers are connected by fine, invisible, lines or webs of qi. The center of your palms are also connected by qi lines through the Laogong energy gates in the middle of the palm. As the hands and fingers open, it may feel like your fingers are expanding and lengthening. By expanding your qi fingers a little, the qi between the hands can become stronger and more powerful.

Continue the open and close movements. Gently expand your arms, from the elbows. Your shoulders and shoulder blades also follow the elbows in opening and closing.

During your practice, you can continue to hold your hands in front of Duqi (Lower Dantian), or raise up your qi arms to the Middle or Upper Dantian and practice Open and Close there.

Variations on Open and Close

1. Open and Close Merges with the Qi Body

Once you have a stronger sensation of qi between the hands, you can practice merging this with body's inner space — that is, the feeling between the hands goes into the body's inner space. The whole qi body is opening and closing along with the elbows and palms.

2. Open and Close in the Three Dantians

Another way to practice Open and Close is by focusing on the three Dantians. Each Dantian alternates being the center. You can start with the qi feeling between the hands going deep into Lower Dantian. Open the Lower Dantian to the whole body, to the qi field, then to the universe, and notice how strong the qi is. Likewise, practice this with your focus and hands on the Middle and Upper Dantians as the center.

3. Healing Open and Close

If you would like to use Open and Close for healing, focus on the inner space of the area of your body that you want to heal. Open that space, then close and gather qi into that space. Open and Close is a very fundamental and effective healing method. When Open and Close is practiced in a Mingjue state, it is a high-level form of Mingjue Healing.

Breathing with Open and Close

When you practice Open and Close, there is no need to combine this with Universal Breathing. Of course, you can combine them, and it can be a very powerful practice. You can choose either to coordinate Open and Close with your breathing, or not. If you choose to coordinate them, **the movements of the hands follows your breathing**, not the other way around — this makes the open and close movements of the hands and arms passive (secondary) to Mingjue and qi body breathing, rather than active (primary). This also helps to keep your breath relaxed.

If you are practicing Open and Close faster than your natural breath and try to coordinate them, your breathing can become too rough, too fast. There is no need to rush. The movement of Open and Close is slow, natural, and relaxed.

The Practice: Open and Close in the Three Dantians

Hold a big qi ball in front of the Lower Dantian.

Soften your gaze. Draw your consciousness back to the center of your head.

Deep inside, the Lower Dantian is empty and open. Observe the internal pure space of the Lower Dantian — it is pure emptiness. The whole universe is also qi. There is no form or matter any more.

Feel the awakening consciousness of Mingjue opening and expanding from Lower Dantian space. Do not mind the sensations of qi. Qi naturally follows Mingjue to open and close.

As Lower Dantian qi opens and expands, this leads the qi palms to open and expand, leading bodily qi to merge out into the qi universe.

Mingjue closes. Mingjue has the information to close, and the focus of Mingjue is deep inside the Lower Dantian. Universal qi follows and penetrates deep inside. Qi palms follow and close.

In this relaxed state, practice Open and Close for a while. Mingjue merges with Lower Dantian to ever subtler levels. Open… close….

Kai He
Open Close

When you are ready, slowly raise your hands to the Middle Dantian space, and observe Middle Dantian space deeply. Relax. Empty. Open…close…open…close…. Totally relax, as though the movements of Open and Close are happening without any effort.

Mingjue remains very clear. The pure movement of the empty space appears in Mingjue. The Middle Dantian and the universe become one.

In this relaxed state, practice Open and Close for a while. Mingjue merges with Middle Dantian to a very subtle level.

When you are ready, slowly raise your hands to the Upper Dantian space. Open…close…open…close….

Observe to a deeper level. If you lose yourself or your mind wanders, do not judge yourself. Just observe again. And experience the emptiness. Totally relax.

With gentle inner smile, notice how the inner space of the Upper Dantian is a pure universal space. The Upper Dantian becomes very light. The Upper Dantian and the universe become one.

In this relaxed state, practice Open and Close for a while. Mingjue merges with Upper Dantian to ever subtler levels.

When you are ready, lower your hands to the Middle Dantian again. Notice how the Middle Dantian is so pure and empty. Open…close…open…close….

Then lower your hands to the Lower Dantian space and observe inside, deeper and deeper. Empty…. Feel how Mingjue is in the Lower Dantian space. Open…close…open…close….

Bring the movements to stillness, holding palms in front of Lower Dantian. Realize that you are pure Mingjue. You are the pure observer. Mind nothing else.

In the Mingjue state, the arms slowly lift qi up (lift the qi ball between the palms) to above the head, then pour qi down through Baihui. Qi pours down through the Upper Dantian, neck, Middle Dantian, to Lower Dantian. Mingjue goes through the whole internal space of the body.

Place the palms on Duqi. Observe the qi body breathing. Then separate your hands to the sides. Slowly restore your gaze.

Variations

- For a stronger practice, try Open and Close while doing Standing Meditation (description follows).

- Open and Close Healing — as your palms hold a qi ball, direct them to a place of your body that needs healing. Then practice Open and Close in that place.

STANDING MEDITATION

Key Points

- Gather qi into Mingmen Inner Palace
- Gather qi into Lower Dantian space (also Middle and Upper Dantians)

Standing Meditation can quickly strengthen internal qi. In general, Standing Meditation is more powerful to increase internal qi than sitting meditations. And when internal qi is strong, the physical body is healthy. Internal qi correlates with vitality.

Standing Meditation forms an entirety state where the Lower Dantian becomes the center of the entire qi universe.

Standing Meditation is **the most effective method for improving the immune system**, more effective than Method One, Lift Qi Up Pour Qi Down, and and Method Two, Body Mind Method.

How to Practice

Start with your feet together. Then separate them by "stepping on qi." This means the feet stay connected to the earth — do not lift them off the ground — as you slowly slide the feet in zigzag fashion until they are shoulder-width apart and parallel.

In the standing position, the center of the feet should be shoulder-width apart. The heels can be a little wider so your toes are pointed inward (slightly pigeon-toed), or you can keep the feet parallel.

Squat down a little while you lift up Baihui and tuck the tailbone under. The connection between Baihui and Huiyin forms a qi channel: the Middle Channel. As the Baihui is lifted upward, the Middle Channel is also lifted upward, in turn lifting up Huiyin from the inside. Take care not to contract Huiyin — just lift it up from inside the Middle Channel by lifting up Baihui. You can imagine there is a line from Baihui to Huiyin. When you lift up Baihui, this will naturally lift up Huiyin from the inside. Always keep this line straight and upright.

Tailbone tucked under: The tailbone draws downward and slightly under, so Mingmen and the whole lumbar spine open. It is as if Duqi presses the Lower Dantian space back toward Mingmen.

Holding a qi ball: Your hands and arms hold a qi ball. Raise the qi ball to the front of your chest. During Standing Meditation, you can move the qi ball to find a comfortable position, at any position between the shoulders and Duqi, not higher or lower.

Everybody's qi is different, so find the level that is optimal for you — wherever you can be more relaxed and feel the entirety more. Allow your body's internal qi state to determine the height of your arms and hands.

When your qi becomes stronger, you will be able to raise your arms higher. Sometimes during the practice, you may need to lower them for a while.

Three Key Elements to Standing Meditation

1. Keep Baihui and Huiyin in a single straight line. Keep this line lifted upward. The whole qi body is centered and straight in posture.

2. Lift up Baihui and draw the tailbone downward, opening the spine. Stretch and expand the whole qi spine.

3. Duqi presses the Lower Dantian space back toward Mingmen, and Mingmen naturally moves backward.

In a good Standing Meditation posture, qi arrives from the three centers into the Lower Dantian (this practice is also called Three Centers Merge):

- From the Baihui — qi pours down from the universe through **Baihui**, down the Middle Channel, to the Lower Dantian. It comes down not through a small line but through a big qi column.

- From the center of the palms — qi enters through the energy point called **Laogong** in the center of the palms, then through the large inner space of the arms all the way down to the Lower Dantian.

- From deep within the earth — earth qi goes through the center of the soles through the energy point called **Yongquan**, then through the inner empty space of the legs, up to the Lower Dantian.

In Mingjue Gongfu, consciousness observes qi of the three centers going to Lower Dantian, then stays in the Lower Dantian space and sleeps there.

The Practice

Place your feet together. Your body is centered and upright. Soften your gaze. With gentle and deep breathing, observe the inner space of your whole qi body. Feel the qi body expanding and becoming bigger and bigger.

Stepping on qi, adjust your feet until the Yongquan energy points in the middle of your soles are shoulder-width apart. Open a little the distance between the heels or keep your feet parallel.

Relax. Observe and feel the qi body as it begins deep and gentle breathing. Through the in-and-out movements of the breath, observe down to deeper levels within, as if you are observing the space within the atoms. Observe deeper and deeper: you are pure qi and the qi space of the body is totally open. Your qi body merges with universal space.

Slowly rotate the qi shoulders, front – upward – backward – downward – and totally relax. Continue to feel the qi body's inner space as empty and how the qi space of the shoulders is rotating, leading the whole body qi to move together as one — in unity.

Feel the qi moving and flowing in the qi arms, chest, Lower Dantian, legs, spine, and head. Slowly and gently, experience the expansion of the qi body. Feel the qi field around you. The internal movement of qi merges with the space around you, connects with the universe, and connects deep inside the earth.

Slowly turn the qi hands to face each other, cupping the palms to hold a qi ball at the level of Duqi. Expand the inner space of the qi arms and fingers, and slowly raise up the qi ball. At the same time, draw the tailbone down and squat a little. The tailbone draws the spine downward as the upper body lifts up from bahui. Feel the whole spine extend, lengthen, expand, and straighten.

Slowly raise the qi ball in front of your body. Find the best height for you, not lower than Duqi or higher than the shoulders.

Observe your qi body's posture and your consciousness.

Gently raise the inner space of the head — but do not use physical power. Instead, feel within the head that a very gentle qi power is pushing Baihui upward with an inner smile. Tuck the chin in. Feel the spine lengthen. Open the cervical vertebrae and observe it as an empty qi space. The inner space of the cervical vertebrae connects with your brain's inner space and Baihui. Open Yintang and feel Yintang's inner space just posterior to the Yintang energy point. Smile into the Shenji Palace and the Upper Dantian space. Feel your brain becoming very relaxed.

The upper and lower teeth connect as if they "touch but don't touch" — it is very gentle. When the qi of the teeth connect this way, the qi will go into your bones — this is good for the kidneys.

If you produce saliva, just swallow. This saliva is very good medicine, very good energy.

The tip of the tongue touches the upper palate, just behind the two front upper teeth. Touch gently, as if they touch but don't touch. The head's inner space gently expands.

Relax. Relax the shoulders. Open the elbows and raise them, feeling how the qi of your arms, heart, chest, and lungs opens. Hold a big qi ball between the arms. Open the fingers, as if the inner space of the fingers has an expansive power. The qi expands to the tips of the fingers. Relax.

If your arms become tired, you can lower them a little, adjusting the height between Duqi and the shoulders.

Relax the spine joint by joint. Relax the tailbone downward. Tuck the tailbone under, as if sitting on a qi chair. As you draw down the tailbone, continue lifting up Baihui, lengthening and emptying the spine. This experience is very gentle — do not use strong force. The inner space of the spine has a slight qi feeling, as if it lengthens both upward and downward.

Gently and slightly draw Duqi backward. Feel how the Lower Dantian space is pushing your Mingmen backward. Observe how the tailbone also pushes Mingmen backward as you tuck it in, opening Mingmen and the lumbar vertebrae.

Lift up Huiyin and gently contract the anus and genitals. Feel the connection between Baihui and Huiyin forming the Middle Channel. Throughout this practice, keep this line straight and upright.

Relax the hips and empty the inner space of the hip joints. Relax the thighs, the knees, calves, ankles, and the feet. Observe the whole qi body and relax.

Observe that the weight of the body is evenly distributed. Your qi legs and qi feet go deep into the qi earth. Earth qi naturally rises and goes through the legs and throughout the whole qi body. Relax.

In this good Standing Meditation posture, Mingjue observes how qi comes from the three centers* (Baihui, Laogong in the palms, and Yongquan in the soles) to the Lower Dantian. Mingjue observes Lower Dantian breathing. Mingjue sleeps in Lower Dantian.

---

* When you are starting out, practice qi from the three centers going to the Lower Dantian, one center at a time. Once you have mastered this step, go to the next level by practicing qi from the three centers going to the Lower Dantian at the same time.

To finish Standing Meditation, slowly lift up the whole qi body from Baihui to a normal standing posture. Close your feet by stepping on qi; do not allow the feet to leave the floor. Still holding the qi ball in front of you, slowly raise the arms to lift qi, the hands raising above the head. Pour qi down through Baihui, Upper Dantian, neck, Middle Dantian, Lower Dantian. Place your hands on Duqi. Lower the hands to your sides. Slowly restore your gaze, rotate your shoulders, and move your body.

Variations on Standing Meditation

Practice Throat Breathing during Standing Meditation, combining it with Lower Dantian Breathing. Feel how Throat Breathing happens from the center of Lower Dantian (the Lower Dantian is the driving force of Throat Breathing).

Homework

- Review the details of the Standing Meditation posture.

- Adjust your posture in a qi state and observe the inner space of the body one segment at a time. In the end, feel how Lower Dantian Breathing becomes Qi Body Breathing.

- Review and practice Universe Breathing. Enjoy the infinite universe breathing.

STRAIGHT LEG SITTING

Key Points

- Enhance the innate qi of Mingmen Inner Palace
- Loosen the lower back and gather qi into spine
- Increase flexibility of the lower spine
- Strengthen central nervous system
- Integrate the body's internal qi (which can be scattered) into Mingmen
- Connect Mingjue to Mingmen Inner Palace

Ming means "life" or "life force." *Men* means "gate." So *Mingmen* means "the gate of life."

A very powerful practice is saying ü inside Mingmen Inner Palace. In Mingmen Inner Palace, we can activate and nourish innate qi — the root of life.

Straight Leg Sitting can gather qi into the central nervous system and the inner space of the spine, down into the inner palace of Mingmen.

Combining Mingjue state with this Mingmen Inner Palace practice can:

- Improve consciousness to a high level
- Nourish the root of life and improve health

These two forces work together, mutually enhancing the other toward a high-level state of being.

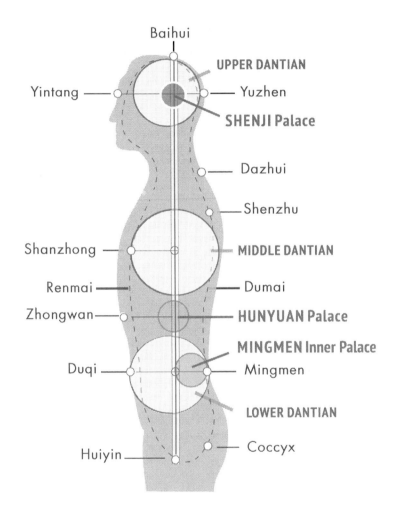

In the diagram above, the Lower Dantian is depicted as a big circle. Within the Lower Dantian and toward the back, there is a small circle — this is the Mingmen Inner Palace, which sits in front of Mingmen, an energy point along the lumbar spine.

Mingmen Inner Palace includes the qi of the kidneys. It holds innate qi, the pure qi passed down by your parents, the pure qi from which life and growth begin. During an individual's life processes, this qi changes because of the hunhua (merge and transform) process. When a high-level consciousness connects to this space, the qi of Mingmen Inner Palace can, in turn, support the high-level consciousness.

Three Levels of Straight Leg Sitting

- Rigid force

- Hidden force

- Transforming force

Only rigid force, the first level, is covered in the general Mingjue Gongfu course. It must be practiced well in order to advance to the other levels. Most people today only practice the rigid force level.

How to Practice Straight Leg Sitting

There are five basic steps to practice the rigid force level of Straight Leg Sitting:

Ming Men Nei Qiao

1. Go into Mingmen inner space and engage in Mingmen Breathing

2. Gather and concentrate qi from three directions into Mingmen

3. Practice sounds into Mingmen inner space

4. Contract from the hips, thighs, knees, and feet

5. Contract from the legs and arms

You may choose to sit on the floor, a bed or mat, or two chairs facing each other.

Straighten your legs in front of you, together. Lift your toes up and toward your body, while gently extending your heels away from the body. Give your legs a little stretch.

Place the palms of your hands on your knees. Hollow your arm pits. Tuck in your chin, gently lifting up bahui. Lift up the base of the ears (the lower part where the ears connect near the jaw).

Then lean your head forward and relax the whole upper body. When you relax the upper body, the weight of the upper body draws downward, naturally pushing Mingmen backward.

Keep this basic posture.

The Practice

Suggestion: You can start the following practice for 5-10 minutes, then increase it to 20-30 minutes over time.

Keeping the basic Straight Leg Sitting posture, follow along with this meditation:

Relax your gaze. Go to the Shenji Palace and observe the whole body. Relax — especially your upper body. The weight of your upper body draws downward, into the inner palace of Mingmen.

Turn your inner gaze to the inner palace of Mingmen and observe. Listen inside Mingmen Inner Palace. Breathe into Mingmen Inner Palace. Feel yourself breathing into that space.

Inhale, drawing qi into Mingmen Inner Palace and feeling it expand. Then exhale, feeling Mingmen Inner Palace contract. Continue this Mingmen Breathing and observe the continuous expansion and contraction.

Some of you may experience the opposite: contraction of Mingmen Inner Palace while inhaling and expansion when exhaling. Others may have other different experiences. Just observe your experience.

The Mingmen inner space is very pure. When you go into that space, feel that it is a big, empty space.

Become aware of your Pure Consciousness. Mingjue merges with Mingmen Inner Palace and with its pure innate qi — from there, Mingjue connects with Mingjue Entirety. Mingjue stays in that space. Mingjue sleeps there.

Mind your posture and adjust it as needed — straighten your legs, keep the toes raised and pointed toward the body, relax your upper body, feel Mingmen pushing backward. Connect with Mingmen Breathing. This is the basic practice. Relax into this posture.

When you have finished your practice, slowly raise the upper body a little. Say ń… ń… ń… (repeat this sound many times). Be aware that you are the pure Mingjue — the independent Mingjue and the Mingjue Entirety.

Then hold a qi ball in front of Duqi, lifting qi up above the head. Pour qi down through the Upper Dantian, neck, Middle Dantian, and Lower Dantian. Place palms on Duqi. Feel the Lower Dantian breathing. Separate hands to the sides. Slowly restore your gaze.

Note: When you feel this breathing very clearly in the Straight Leg Sitting posture, you can practice Mingmen Breathing for a long time: one month, two months, or a year. Just sit and feel Mingmen Inner Palace, how consciousness goes inside

Mingmen and sleeps there, breathes there. When you come to feel Mingmen breathing very well, this practice can greatly benefit you.

Advanced Practice

When you can feel Mingmen inner space breathing very well, repeat the above Straight Leg Sitting practice, but with the following additional breathing elements.

The breathing method described below can also be practiced in the simple, relaxed sitting posture, as well as Standing Meditation.

Inhalation: When you inhale, draw in air through the Heavenly Gate, down into Mingmen. At the same time, contract Huiyin and Duqi into the inner palace of Mingmen. Feel qi from the Baihui draw down through the diaphragm and into Mingmen Inner Palace. This is a powerful way to increase the qi inside the Mingmen Inner Palace.

Important: Duqi and Huiyin draw in and up, and the diaphragm goes downward. So with each inhalation, feel how the pressure inside Mingmen increases. This pushes backward the lumbar vertebrae and the low back, and opens up the lumbar vertebrae. Also feel qi entering the inner space of the spine.

There are two sources of power that work together:

• From Mingmen Inner Palace — when the abdomen draws inward, so qi is drawn into Mingmen.

• From Duqi — when the lower abdomen contracts and sends qi backward, so qi is pushed into Mingmen.

The qi from Duqi going into Mingmen mainly comes from food — hence, it is called **acquired qi**. The energy from food is concentrated in the Lower Dantian. When you draw Duqi backward, this Lower Dantian acquired qi goes into Mingmen Inner Palace.

When you draw up Huiyin to Mingmen, this qi is mainly the **essence qi**, or sexual energy. This qi also draws into Mingmen.

The qi from the Heavenly Gate or Baihui mainly comes from the infinite empty space of the universe — or **universal qi**. This qi descends through the Heavenly Gate, to the Upper Dantian, Middle Dantian, and down into Mingmen.

When you breathe in, these three kinds of qi from three directions converge inside Mingmen.

Exhalation: When you exhale, relax. First relax from Mingmen, then from Duqi and Huiyin, then gradually from the hips to the knees, ankles, and toes. The next step is to relax going upward, from the shoulders, elbows, wrists, hands and fingers. This is a process, but it is very fast; it is not easy to distinguish each step from the others.

(Repeat, breathing in and out.)

Mingmen Inner Palace is the center of this practice. It is the center of power.

But remember! Mingjue is the master. Mingjue combines with the breathing, Mingjue is in the breathing, and the breathing is in Mingjue. Both the contraction and release happen in pure Mingjue. Mingjue mainly merges with the qi of Mingmen inner space — as if it is sleeping there. So always keep Mingjue clear during this breathing exercise.

Deepen the Contractions

Once you feel a good facility with combining the sounds with the contractions, you can start to contract more places. Begin with one part, then two, gradually adding more parts:

Duqi contracts. Huiyin contracts. The anus contracts. The hips and thighs contract. The sexual/reproductive organs contract (external and internal organs). The lower abdomen contracts. The buttocks contract. The sides of the waist contract. The ribs contract. Everything contracts toward Mingmen.

Feel the qi — the power of it — going through the qi body and into Mingmen. For example, when you contract the thighs, feel the muscles contract and gather energy into the bones, the bone marrow, and all of it moving into Mingmen. Or, when you contract from the toes, raise your toes and extend the heels outward, curl the toes as you inhale, but draw in from the center of Yongquan (the middle of the soles). When you contract, the power goes into Yongquan. Contract all the muscles in the legs, from feet to thighs, drawing the qi into Mingmen.

When you relax the muscles, relax completely. Suddenly the qi opens through a big qi channel, the qi and blood flowing through the legs to the toes again.

Contract again — toes, ankles, calves, knees, thighs, hips, Huiyin, Duqi — all contract to Mingmen. Qi comes back through the legs to Mingmen. Contract, and suddenly qi comes into Mingmen.

When you practice this method, the legs become very powerful. This can naturally heal all kinds of blockages inside the legs. Some people may feel their legs becoming thinner, lighter, and stronger. Why? Because the qi is gathering into the center (Mingmen).

Mingjue remains clear and playful, even during these powerful contractions, always observing independently, within and throughout the legs and the whole qi body. Once you learn and practice the basics, Mingjue can play with the qi.

Variations on Straight Leg Sitting

- **Throat Breathing** — when you inhale with Throat Breathing, you are drawing qi from the three directions into Mingmen, and from the entire qi body into Mingmen.

- **Holding your breath** — you may hold your breath for a short while, depending on your state.

- **Sleeping in Mingmen** — if you feel tired after this practice, just rest and go to sleep in Mingmen Inner Palace. Feel Mingjue breathing in Mingmen Inner Palace as you sleep.

- **Adding sound** — when you contract/inhale, you can combine this with the sounds: yun… yun… yun…. When you breathe out and relax: ying. Each successive time you say **yun**, increase the strength of the contraction. At the end of inhaling yun… yun… yun…, hold the qi there for a moment. Then exhale and relax, saying: **ying**. You can say yun slowly or quickly. Notice how making the sounds and breathing, together, can enhance the gathering of qi into Mingmen. These sounds do not have any specific meaning; they can simply help to mobilize qi.

PUSH THE MOUNTAIN

Key Points

- Observation, concentration, relaxation
- Training the independence, power, and stability of Mingjue

Place your feet together. Keep your body centered and upright. Soften your gaze.

With gentle and deep breathing, observe the inner space of the whole qi body. As you feel it, become the qi body and expand the qi body. The qi body becomes bigger and bigger and merges with the universe qi space.

Say ñ… ñ… ñ… (repeat many times) to come to the pure Mingjue state. Relax. Mingjue is in the whole qi body. The qi body is in Mingjue.

Keeping your qi arms straight, slowly raise them from the sides until they are horizontal and parallel with the ground (like a cross or "T"). Then flex the wrists so your palms are "pushing mountains" on each side. Keep your arms straight and relaxed. Keep a smile on your face.

Say ñ silently, keeping Mingjue clear and stable. ñ… ñ… ñ….

The feeling of your arms is reflected in Mingjue; the arms are in Mingjue. ñ… ñ… ñ….

If you feel pain or heaviness in your arms, Mingjue receives this information but remains clear — do not attach to the feelings, just observe them. Observe your Mingjue as independent from the body, even as Mingjue is in the body. Do not return to the habit of losing yourself to the physical sensations. Stay relaxed with an inner smile. Say ñ into the inner space of the arms.

Stay in this posture for 7 or 10 minutes. Gradually increase the time as your gongfu improves. If you can practice this for an hour, Mingjue will very powerful!

When you are ready, slowly lower down the arms. Rotate the shoulders with gentle and deep breathing. Mingjue merges with the whole qi body but keeps its independence from the state in the body. The body remains centered with Mingjue as the master.

MINGJUE HEALING PRACTICES

Mingjue Healing* is a form of Mingjue Gongfu. That means that, when Mingjue sends information to do a healing, you are also training and developing your Mingjue. If your Mingjue goes deeper and deeper while keeping the healing intention clear and relaxed, your Mingjue state improves, Mingjue naturally becomes more confident, and the healing becomes more effective.

Your primary focus is on Mingjue itself. In Mingjue Healing, do not focus on the problem or the patient. Rather, focus on the healthy information in Mingjue. The healthy Mingjue information merges with the space you want to heal and merges into the qi universe. This is very subtle. Repeatedly review this information until you understand it.

Important: You must ask this question in your mind, again and again:

What is the basic health entirety state?

Answer: pure Mingjue love, peace, happiness, gratitude

Mingjue Healing has no specific methods. You can use your hands, you can do La Qi, you can give a massage — there is no conflict with any of these methods. What makes it Mingjue Healing is that you remain in the Mingjue state. Even when you visualize, the visualization happens in the Mingjue state.

Trust is paramount. To have a good healing, you must trust the Mingjue Entirety, and the person you are healing must trust you. If you feel that this basic health entirety state is not sufficient, Teacher Wei recommends practicing other methods first: visualizing pure light, doing dynamic methods, repeating sound practices, breathing practices, Open and Close — then returning to Mingjue Healing when your trust is stronger.

Teacher Wei's healing method: "I just stay in Pure Consciousness state, receiving pure information from the consciousness field and sending it to the other person. In my consciousness, she is qi. I stay in a deep Mingjue consciousness state and merge with her qi body. Her qi body is in my Mingjue. Just gently giving information: 'Inside qi is open and flowing well, all blockages have already disappeared.' Very simple."

The Practice for Self-Healing

Sit or lie in a comfortable posture. Relax the gaze. Repeat ñ to come to deeper Mingjue state. ñ… ñ… ñ…. Mingjue goes throughout your body.

---

* For more details on Mingjue Healing, please review the theory of Mingjue Healing in Part I of this book.

Observe the area you want healing. Mingjue goes into that space, deeper and deeper. Relax. Feel Mingjue inside that space and know that area is transforming, healing. The deeper the Mingjue state you achieve, the deeper you penetrate that space. Say ñ... ñ... ñ.... Feel how your Mingjue merges with the world consciousness field and with the universe. Say ñ... ñ... ñ.... Feel this space harmonizing with universal qi in the awakening entirety. In the entirety state, focus on the healthy information within your Mingjue — universal love. Say ñ... ñ... ñ.... Send the good information of ñ to the place that needs healing. You want to change that space — that is your deep intention. Now relax the intention. Feel Mingjue coming to a deeper level, and feel your Mingjue information becoming more powerful. Trust that the healing is already happening. Relax your Mingjue. Relax and focus at the same time. Feel that your intention to heal is within Mingjue. Trust this healthy information, the healthy state in your Mingjue. Open more. Relax. Repeat ñ... ñ... ñ.... Stay relaxed.

Say ñ with a Mingjue healing intention for five minutes, thirty minutes, or one hour.

When you are finished, hold a qi ball with your palms in front of Duqi. Slowly lift qi up to above the head, then pour qi down through the head, neck, chest, abdomen.

Place hands on Duqi.

Rest there for a while.

Restore your gaze.

MINGJUE EMOTIONAL HEALING PRACTICE

Come to a good Mingjue state. Stay in the Mingjue state, stay in Mingjue love. Empty yourself, empty your mind… n… n… n…. You are pure Mingjue.

Accept your past, everything in the past, even emotional traumas or blockages.

Accept the reason or cause of the emotional traumas or blockages.

Accept your emotions.

Accept the people who triggered the emotions.

And love them all.

Say the mantra:

I am Mingjue love.

　　I am Mingjue peace.

　　　　I am Mingjue happiness.

　　　　　　I am Mingjue gratitude.

Repeat this many times.

Then:

We are Mingjue love.

　　We are Mingjue peace.

　　　　We are Mingjue happiness.

　　　　　　We are Mingjue gratitude.

The Mingjue collective field sustains you.

All the past is already past — this is all just information that has gotten fixed in your mind.

Enjoy this present moment.

Emotional Healing in Hun Yuan Palace

There are three palaces inside the body (you can review the diagram at the start of Part 2, Key Energy Gates and Points):

1. Shenji Palace — the house of consciousness

2. Hun Yuan Palace — convergence of the five organ systems; can transform emotions and the functioning of the organ systems

3. Mingmen Inner Palace — house of innate bodily qi; is the root of other palaces

While focusing into Hun Yuan Palace, you can practice the four-part emotional healing mantra of **ho'oponono**:

> *I'm sorry, please forgive me, thank you, I love you.*
> *I'm sorry, please forgive me, thank you, I love you….*

When you transform and heal one relationship, you heal them all — because you yourself are healed, which then affects all your relationships in this life, in the past, and in the future.

When you experience deep healing, you can then simplify the mantra:

> *Thank you, I love you….*

Additional Practices for Emotional Transformation

As a general rule, sound practices are better at transforming the qi of internal organs, where emotions are stored. The following methods are good for working on emotions at the level of energy or qi:

1. Happiness or laughter qigong — watch fun videos or play joyful music.

2. Inner Smile practice — in the Mingjue state, smile inwardly at the places you want clearing or transforming.

3. Five Organ Sound Healing (part of Zhineng Qigong Level 3 Method)

4. "Heng Ha!" This phrase is two generals commanding the body and its emotions, like they are saying, "Cheer up! Emotional blockages disappear!" With "Heng!," feel the Lower Dantian space expand. With "Ha!," the lower dantain energy opens up the middle and Upper Dantian spaces. "Heng Ha" can also trigger Mingjue consciousness to awaken.

5. Throat Breathing (during Standing Meditation or seated) — use deeper and stronger breathing to open up the blockages more quickly. Consciousness and breathing combine together to go through the organs and areas of tension.

Throat Breathing is especially powerful for clearing the upper and lower airways, so this is **good for strengthening the immune system**. This is also **good for transforming the grief carried in the lungs and chest**.

For emotional trauma: Trauma lies deeper and subtler than emotions that are at the qi level — **trauma is at the level of information**. To heal and transform emotional trauma, you need to practice the Mingjue Entirety state to see through the trauma and understand it.

In a good Mingjue state, say the following lines to the causes of the trauma, as well as to the trauma itself (which people can grow to hate and resent):

> *I'm sorry.*
> > *Please forgive me.*
> > > *Thank you.*
> > > > *I love you.*

If you repeat this mantra over and over again, one day this new information will harmonize with the old information, and the trauma will be transformed.

This mantra can even be practiced by those who don't know Mingjue or who aren't in a peaceful observer's state. You can simply connect deep within your heart and say the four-part mantra above as it is.

From a Mingjue level, the information can also be the following four sentences:

> *I am Mingjue love.*
> > *I am Mingjue peace.*
> > > *I am Mingjue happiness.*
> > > > *I am Mingjue gratitude.*

Homework

In Mingjue Entirety state, remember and observe your past history in chronological order. Go through as many memories as you can. Remember all the experiences — both difficult and happy.

Accept and love all the happy things.

Accept and love all the challenging things.

Stay in the Mingjue love state.

Remind yourself that none of these things are your pure Mingjue. They are just information. Mingjue observes them, reflects them, and loves them all from a place of harmonious Mingjue Entirety.

Keep this state: "No problem!"

SUPER ABILITIES PRACTICES

Note: Teacher Wei recommends, as you're beginning, not to practice these super abilities methods for too long. Start with 20 or 30 minutes, then gradually increase as you continue to develop your consciousness and abilities. This can provide time to ground and integrate the information and energies. After each practice, he recommends other dynamic methods in the Mingjue state to further ground and integrate.

Super abilities reflect the potential of Mingjue. They are also a function of Mingjue. So these methods can help to further develop and stabilize Mingjue.

If you forget Mingjue when you develop super abilities, it is easy to lose yourself. Mingjue can lose itself on these functions and you can risk feeling special. At this point, you are limiting your life and your potential.

The super abilities framework is one that is more expanded than the ordinary framework. But Mingjue ability is still higher and purer. Everyone has access to Mingjue. Anyone can develop Mingjue's functions. So when you experience super abilities, you are experiencing everyone and anyone's potential. Realizing this can help you keep the pride of specialness from becoming an obstruction.

> Everyone has the same potential
> to develop both
> Mingjue and super abilities.

The functions of Mingjue are to receive and send information.

Receiving Information

- By opening Yintang, you can see your body's inner states and situations.

- By opening Tianmen, you can experience direct knowing.

Sending Information

- When you can visualize deep change within your body, you can manifest these changes more powerfully.

- The function of visualization is to change yourself and others; visualization is a way of sending information to create something new.

Mingjue Opens Tianmen, Heavenly Gate

When you practice the following methods, consciousness becomes very focused on the head and brain. For those who experience intense sensations or emotions or thoughts, remember to use **Mingjue to observe the qi brain** — and observe it with Mingjue love. Say xü to empty and transform the space. Also, relax your intention. This can help to lessen the intensity.

Note: The following four methods are connected. They are four steps of one practice.

Method 1

From Baihui, move slightly forward and look for a place that is slightly deeper, hollow, or softer. This point is the center of Tianmen ("Heavenly Gate"). Gently press your fingers and shake or vibrate to open Tianmen. Make this hollow, visualizing it opening down and sending qi to Shenji Palace.

The middle fingers on both hands come together and depress the center of Tianmen — meaning the backs of the fingers come together at the top of your head. Alternatively, you can use just one hand.

Method 2

Place the palms together, facing downward toward your scalp, hovering slightly above the head.

Draw the hands up and down, up and down, up and down, visualizing and feeling qi moving through Tianmen to Shenji Palace.

At the end of this practice, your hands come down over Tianmen, pouring qi down over the face and chest, and into Hun Yuan Palace. Place your hands over Hun Yuan Palace.

Rest there for a while. Then separate your hands.

Method 3

From Shenji Palace, visualize light or qi moving up toward Tianmen.

Make the sound **ga-er**, which can help to mobilize qi. Observe Tianmen opening from Shenji Palace, so you can see the sky from within your head.

With the sound ga-er, the vibrations can break up blockages in Tianmen. Say the sounds gently or silently. If repeated too strongly, you might experience some dizziness or disequilibrium. Mostly, you are using your consciousness to loosen the blockages, rather than the sound itself. You may feel Tianmen tingling or buzzing.

Method 4

Repeat the phrase: **Shenji ling kong** with each exhalation. *Shenji* vibrates inside Shenji Palace. *Ling kong* surges up toward the sky through Tianmen.

Use consciousness information to form a qi column to open up the space. When you breathe in, maintain the qi column (don't lower it down). When you breathe out and say shenji ling kong, raise the qi column higher. Maintain that height, observe the whole qi column while breathing in. So the end effect is that the qi column continues to get higher with each subsequent breath.

Keep the qi column erect; do not have it leaning forward, backward, or to either side. Mingjue observes and directs this from within Shenji Palace.

Then the qi column lowers down to Hun Yuan Palace. Observe the whole body and qi column. Mingjue sleeps inside Hun Yuan Palace.

From Hun Yuan Palace, Mingjue expands to the whole qi universe. And from the whole universe, Mingjue draws back again into Hun Yuan Palace. Inside Hun Yuan Palace, it is a pure, empty state. Rest there for a while.

Important: Rest in Hun Yuan Palace or Mingmen Inner Palace.

After practicing super abilities in Shenji Palace, opening Tianmen or opening Yintang, bring down your consciousness to Hun Yuan Palace or Mingmen Inner Palace — either is fine.

Questions on Opening Tianmen

Q: Does it matter if we notice the column of light above Tianmen being stronger on one side than the other? Should we try to balance it out?

A: This doesn't matter a lot. Everyone's right- and left-sided qi is a little different. Just observe it. Don't fall into the habit of following or getting attached to the qi sensations. Instead, use Mingjue to visualize a straight qi column above Tianmen. Mainly focus on consciousness, rather than qi. **It is actually a consciousness column more than a qi column.**

Q: What do you suggest if we feel our consciousness rising up and expanding out during the practice, which can feel strong and unsettling?

A: This happens when our consciousness is very strongly bound to our body's qi, so when the qi rises, consciousness goes along with it. When the qi goes up, connect to Mingjue; Mingjue can observe and gently reduce the surge of power. Don't make the power too strong. Try to find the middle point. This is common with both Tianmen and Yintang practices.

Q: What if there is no column of light, no column that we visualize, or no column to lengthen — that our experience is just opening of Tianmen directly into the vast universe?

A: This does not matter. The intention is simply to open up your consciousness to information. If there is information in your consciousness, that's all that matters. There is no need for the sensations or visualizations to be very clear. Simply notice, Who is opening Tianmen and Yintang? Who is observing from Shenji Palace? Then you are gradually becoming your own life master.

> When we open
> to the universe,
> we receive good
> universal medicine.

MINGJUE OPENS SHENJI PALACE AND YINTANG

Use your hands to send qi to Yintang. Overlap your palms in front of and facing Yintang. Gently draw closer toward Yintang, close to the skin but not touching.

Then draw qi out, one to two feet, then draw it closer again, close to Yintang but not touching.

Relax Yintang. Observe inside your forehead that it becomes empty and light. Repeat the in-and-out movement of the palms. Qi goes in and out.

When you are done, lower the hands down to Hun Yuan Palace. Relax Hun Yuan Palace, then rest the palms there for a while.

Note: A powerful way to focus your consciousness is to observe the tip of the nose. Then move consciousness from there to Yintang.

RIGHT ANGLE BREATHING

Observe Shenji Palace. Then observe the right angle qi channels: in front through Yintang, and above through Baihui.

Breathe in through Yintang to Shenji Palace, then breathe out through Baihui.

With the next inhalation, reverse the breathing pattern: draw consciousness down through Baihui, then breathe out through Yintang.

Repeat this slowly and gently.

When you have that basic breath down, begin making a small loop (consciousness observes or visualizes this qi loop) in Shenji Palace whenever you breathe in and draw qi to Shenji Palace.

So the basic movement: breathe in through Yintang to Shenji Palace, make a small loop in Shenji Palace, then breathe out through Baihui. Reverse the direction as you draw consciousness down through Baihui, make a small loop in Shenji Palace, then breathe out through Yintang.

Note: The small loop in Shenji Palace is actually a small qi ball — so you can visualize Mingjue turning the qi ball when you make the loop. Make it playful!

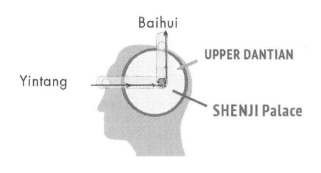

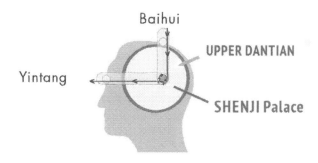

MINGJUE HEALING LOVE LIGHT ROTATION

After practicing some of the above methods for super abilities, consciousness can become very focused, powerful, and more open. In this state, you can practice this healing love light rotation.

This healing should be done in the Mingjue state — Mingjue as universal love.

Begin by observing the Yintang inner space, just posterior to the Yintang energy point between the eyebrows. Some of you can perceive or feel light inside the Yintang space. For those who cannot yet perceive the light, begin with visualizing it: sunlight streaming from Yintang inner space into Shenji Palace.

You can envision what sunlight looks like when reflected on a mirror — very clear and bright, transmitting happy, healing information.

Once you can visualize or perceive the light in the head's inner space, your consciousness can readily merge with light (or sunlight) from above your head, drawing it down through Baihui as a spiral. Mingjue begins to rotate this healing and happy light — **first counterclockwise**, going down through Baihui, inward into Shenji Palace.

The light rotation spreads down throughout the whole body. Mingjue guides the spiral slowly through each body part. The light rotates with universal, unconditional love and transforms the whole body, part by part — from the head to the feet. Feel the transformation.

The light itself is a very powerful energy. In addition, **the rotation taps into the rotation of the galaxy**. Together, they merge — hunhua — and synergize!

Repeat the spiral from the head to the feet, this time, in a clockwise direction, slowly, methodically, practicing observation, concentration, and relaxation.

Repeat the counterclockwise, then clockwise rotations several times.

When you are done, hold a qi ball and lift qi up to above the head. Pour qi down from Baihui through the Upper Dantian, Middle Dantian, and place hands over Hun Yuan Palace. Rest there for a while.

MEDITATIONS ON DEATH

There are many different meditations to go into, then beyond, death.

Method 1

To face death, visualize the process of death. When you visualize death, feel that death is just like this visualization. This is a common practice in Buddhist meditation. Soften your gaze. Draw consciousness into Shenji Palace. From there, observe your body.

Slowly, visualize yourself getting logs to create a big fire around you. In the fire, your body becomes ashes. Observe this deeply and slowly. When everything has become ash, a strong wind blows the ash away. Nothing remains.

When you visualize this, notice that the body has disappeared. But where are you? You are observing this entire process, even after the body has totally disappeared. **The observer still remains**.

This meditation cultivates the autonomy of consciousness, because you can observe the process of the physical body disappearing. This observer is you — your consciousness. Through this practice, you can realize, "The observer is me."

Method 2

Visualize a dead body. Visualize the process of decomposition in detail. Apply your imagination with as much detail as you can to the process of decomposition.

Observe how the original beauty of the physical form vanishes. Observe the unpleasant odor, all other unpleasant processes that the body undergoes. Observe the tissues disappearing and the bones that remain. Observe the bones in detail.

Over time with this meditation, you may experience that your attachment to the physical body gradually lessens and disappears.

Method 3

This is the Mingjue practice — the direct way to go beyond the body. Why? Because when you come to Mingjue state, you realize that, if you are Mingjue, you are not your body. Mingjue is autonomous and does not experience death.

Your body is like your house: you inhabit it, use it, and take care of it. The body changes every second. Yesterday's body and today's body are not the same. Yesterday, many cells within the body died, and today, many new cells have appeared. In each second, the old self dies and a new self appears.

Every seven years, the entire body and its cells will have completely turned over. This means that every seven years, you become completely new; the old cells will have completely disappeared.

This cycle repeats over and over again. This is just the flow and transformation of life in the present moment.

Mingjue sees through this cycle. If the body changes, Mingjue says, "No problem! I am Mingjue, I am the True Self, I am Yiyuanti. In each present moment, I am the clear and independent existence."

Mingjue remains independent, but freely manages the body in this life, during all of its processes of transformation. The new life is born in Mingjue love information. Mingjue universal love information can go throughout the whole (new) body.

Trust that a new life is already born. Enjoy this process of life.

MINGJUE PRACTICE OVERVIEW

Here is a brief overview of the methods to develop good Mingjue Gongfu:

1. **Come to the Mingjue state and merge with the Mingjue collective consciousness field**. Make this stronger every day.

2. **Improve Mingjue** through simple and direct methods —

   • Train your awareness — this is not a method, but a direct experience. "At this present moment you are the observer, and you are aware of the observer" — this is a very direct way to help Mingjue grow up. Once you have this awareness, just remain there. Can you feel how the observer is in the present moment? Just be the observer. Be in that pure state like a clear mirror. Be totally relaxed.

   • Repeat the sounds — Shenji and ñ. If you are used to saying Shenji and this is better for you, this is a great practice. But for many, saying ñ is the primary method. There is also Lingjue Breathing. All three of these can help you go directly to Mingjue.

3. **Mingjue Entirety and Standing Meditation** — Mingjue stands still yet active, merging with the qi body, then the qi universe, strengthening the Mingjue Entirety. With Throat Breathing, contract qi into Mingmen and nourish the root of life.

4. **Mingjue transforms the body with universal qi** — the dynamic methods are: Open and Close (also called Kai He and La Qi), Push and Pull, and Big Circulation — for detailed instructions on the dynamic movements, please refer to video recordings, live group practices, or Dr. Pang's e-books which are available on www.theworldconsciousnesscommunity.com. If you use these very simple methods to practice Mingjue, and Mingjue transforms qi, you can go very deep. These are very powerful ways to change the body.

5. **Mingjue enhances innate qi and the qi of the spine** — straight Leg Sitting activates and nourishes innate qi in the Mingmen Inner Palace.

6. **Mingjue increases Lower Dantian qi** — this enhances acquired and innate qi together — to, overall making qi more abundant and strengthening the qi of the body more effectively. There are two recommended methods: Standing Meditation and Massaging the Abdomen (Roufu) in a lying posture, where the palms are placed midway between Duqi and the base of the sternum, rotating slowly, methodically, in a clockwise direction — right, up, left, down). When these two methods are practiced in the Mingjue state, you can improve

Mingjue and make qi abundant at the same time.

7. Mingjue strengthens the spine — the two movements are Bow Body, Arch Back and Caterpillar Movement.

8. Mingjue Entirety walking meditation — this can increase the flexibility of Mingjue to be more present in the activities of daily life.

9. Mingjue Entirety lying meditation — Mingjue meditation while lying down can bring you to more comfort and relaxation — and therefore more openness. Lying meditation can help you more readily merge with the universe and recharge inside with universal qi, recovering energy efficiently. Massaging the Abdomen (Roufu) can be done lying down.

SUGGESTIONS FOR DAILY PRACTICE

1. Observe Shenji Palace while repeating the sound Shenji or ñ — 10 minutes. Go as deep as possible.

2. Do Qi Body Breathing — go from head to feet while also observing your breathing. 10 minutes or longer.

3. Practice a dynamic movement method in the Mingjue state — 30 minutes. During the movements, try to maintain deep observation.

4. Observe the inner palace of Mingmen static practice 20 minutes. This is a good practice to do before sleep. Just bring Mingjue to Mingmen Inner Palace and rest there. Do nothing.

5. Practice a walking meditation — walk around your room for at least 5 minutes, maintaining Mingjue awareness. This can help you form a new habit so that, when you move about in your daily life, you can better maintain and connect to this state.

6. Jog or hike or run — practice these active movements with Mingjue awareness to further train your observer — at least 5 minutes.

7. BONUS: "Observe but not observe."

When you have improved the stability and depth of your observation, the next level of practice is to further relax your intention. Try to experience the state of "observing but not observing."

How can you "observe but not observe?" Our language is limited in describing this. Just try to relax into an experience where it seems that all of the following have disappeared: your intention, your thoughts, all stimulation and signals from the nervous system. It might feel like you cannot react at all because you're so relaxed.

For example, when you repeatedly say ñ, at some point this information will appear on its own, silently and gently. Even when you do not consciously say or think ñ, the information is there.

At this level, you have gone beyond the feelings in the body to a deeper state of relaxation and emptiness. When you stop thinking ñ, you are still leaving the information of ñ there. You know ñ is there, but you do not need to consciously think it any more. It becomes a pure state that contains the information of ñ within it.

QI PURIFICATIONS

In qigong, Healing Crises are called *qi reactions* or *qi purifications*. Because these practices can activate powerful transformation of information and energy, reactions can occur more frequently than with other forms of healing. These can be emotional reactions or physical, usually old, subconscious blockages that need to transform. These reactions are normal and are just part of the process of healing.

Two Examples

- When some students practice very deeply inside Hun Yuan Palace in the upper abdomen, this space opens. Subsequently, they may experience significant pain, some sensations in the internal organs, or strong emotions.

- During methods that activate qi flow through the low back and open the lumbar vertebrae, some may not be able to stand back up right away, or they may experience some pain in the tailbone, sacrum, hips, low back, upper back, or neck.

Some students experience more qi reactions than others. The process differs from person to person.

One of Teacher Wei's friends, a fellow student in the master class, had practiced Zhineng Qigong deeply and diligently for more than thirty years. He often experienced the changes in his body's inner space to be very difficult. When one kind of qi reaction disappeared, another deep reaction would follow soon after. Many difficulties came during those thirty years, but he kept a positive state and welcomed the difficulties as change. He continued to practice diligently. Step by step, his body and consciousness changed and he created a new life.

How to Respond to Qi Purifications

1. Repeat the ň sound. With pain, Mingjue can easily lose itself, as the feeling of pain dominates everything. You can, however, directly come back to Mingjue again: ň… ň… ň…!

2. Repeat the xü sound. With any physical sensations, you can say xü into those places and transform them into qi, thinking, "Everything is qi, everything is always changing, merging and transforming in every moment." This practice can help you release any attachments.

3. Maintain the "no problem" state. If the qi body has a reaction, trust and receive this information: "This is a good change. There is no problem. These reactions are normal and are just part of the process of change." Know that it is Mingjue that is providing this good information. Even if the reaction is very painful or strong, recognize that there is a deeper, internal change. For those with very powerful Mingjue states: If pain happens? No problem. If the arms and legs are lost? No problem. Death? No problem. The True Self has no blockages.

4. Remember the body is qi. When qi reactions happen, remember that the body is qi, the sensations are qi, and Mingjue and universal qi are both transforming your qi body. If you remain very stable, you can see the changes happening in the present moment.

5. Observe the power of your Mingjue. Challenges — whether as qi reactions or as experiences in your daily life — come because there are areas of weakness that can be strengthened. If there were no difficulties, you would not be able to train and improve your Mingjue. Sometimes it can be easy to be fooled and think, "My Mingjue is independent and stable now." Then various obstacles occur and you see where your Mingjue still has room to grow up and grow strong. With repeated challenges, the observer comes to knows itself, growing more stable, relaxed, and powerful than before the challenge. Deep inside your heart, everyone has to make the decision: "I want to improve my Mingjue. I will trust." If you have this mindset, your practice will become easier, accepting all kinds of difficulties as good opportunities to practice Mingjue. This is the real power of Mingjue and requires conscious training. (However, if you always have a comfortable state in practice, that is also good — it is beautiful!)

Additional Tips

1. Lighten the practice. Do not practice too hard or long, especially in the beginning. And do not use too much force, especially if you have challenges in the lumbar spine area. If the symptoms are too strong, adjust your breathing practices or contraction efforts to be more gentle. Also, raise your upper body a little more. Gradually, qi becomes more abundant and the qi of the spine and internal organs begins to flow more freely. The pain and other symptoms will lessen and eventually disappear.

2. Use mainly the qi state. Use qi to nourish your spine; the pain can more readily decrease.

3. Go beyond any emotions or pain. If you have strong emotions or pain, do not mind them. Observe them as if you are watching a movie. Experience them but stay grounded as the autonomous observer, separate from the symptoms. The more your mind focuses on and attaches to the symptoms, the more you can become controlled by them. Just focus on Mingjue, go deeper and deeper, relax and surrender more. Gradually the ego or thinking mind will quiet down, and all attachments and fixations will disappear. The emotions and pain will disappear, too.

4. Say ň into places of pain or contraction. If you say ň into a particular place in the body, this is Mingjue Healing. Another way is for Mingjue to go to the place of challenge and send the information of "Haola!" there. The qi blockages can readily disappear.

5. Do Open and Close in that space. Mingjue can guide Open and Close in that place. You can also do Mingjue Breathing into that space to merge and transform the qi. The mind stays clear and pure, not attaching to any of the sensations.

In the history of all the great masters and sages of the world, almost all went through many difficulties before they achieved a high-level, enlightened state.

PRACTICES FOR SPECIFIC
HEALTH CHALLENGES

In Mingjue Gongfu, all the methods referenced below are practiced in the Mingjue Entirety state, to connect to the source of healing. Mingjue Gongfu focuses on healing the entirety (the body as a whole, integrated unit), but sometimes specific movements can have added benefits.

Head and brain conditions: Crane's Head

Spine conditions: Caterpillar Movement, Bow Body/Arch Back

Chest, lungs, heart, breasts, arm conditions: Chen Qi, Open and Close in the Middle Dantian.

Digestive, abdominal, pelvic conditions, and challenges with detoxification (liver, gall bladder, spleen, kidneys): Open and Close, Universal Breathing in the space that has imbalances or blockages. Merge the Lower Dantian space with the inner space of the specific organ or tissue. Also, Hip Rotations, Lower Spine Rotations.

Leg conditions: Bow Body/Arch Back, Caterpillar Movement, or Wall Squats

High blood pressure: Open and Close in the Lower Dantian or Mingmen inner space. Also, Lower Spine Rotations.

Sleep challenges:

- **If due to an overactive mind**: Breathing into Mingmen inner space while counting the breaths, Massaging the Abdomen (Roufu).

- **If due to imbalances in the internal organs**: Breathing so the Middle Dantian qi merges with the Lower Dantian qi; stabilize this entirety, balance the qi of the heart and kidneys.

Q & A WITH TEACHER WEI

1. Do I need to know qigong to practice Mingjue?

Knowledge of qigong is not a prerequisite for Mingjue Gongfu. Mingjue Gongfu includes Mingjue meditations and Zhineng Qigong dynamic methods; the latter are very simple, and therefore easy to learn. You can practice either the Mingjue meditations alone, or combine them with qigong movements — adding the movements is more effective for your body and health. Teacher Wei teaches Mingjue meditations as well as simple and effective Zhineng Qigong practices in the Mingjue Entirety state.

2. How much time do you recommend for us to practice?

The more often, the better. Ideally, you have at least one longer practice session a day. If you have more time, practice longer and deeper. If you do not have longer stretches of time, practice for shorter periods several times a day.

For the best effects, Mingjue practice should be integrated into your daily life. See the events and interactions in your daily life as practice ground for developing and maintaining a stable Mingjue state. Maintaining a stable and centered consciousness state in daily life is the golden key to Mingjue Gongfu. Mingjue will quickly grow up this way.

3. If I don't have enough time to practice all the methods, how do I decide what to prioritize?

This question comes from a mindset that is fixated on the methods. If you observe, go to a deeper level of the entirety, and therefore understand your deeper purpose in practicing, you will realize that you only need to practice a few methods. If you train in the Mingjue Entirety state, that is enough.

The methods taught in Mingjue Gongfu courses by Teacher Wei are simple, and even these can sometimes be too much. You can mix and match the methods from different modules, provided that you have practiced and developed the foundational practices of observation — of the qi body, qi entirety states, and the Mingjue collective consciousness field. The practice of observation can always go deeper and deeper.

Once you have this good foundation, the dynamic methods are practiced within this Mingjue Entirety state. A good and deep transformation will then follow.

4. Why has my sleeping pattern changed?

While repeating Shenji or ñ, your consciousness draws back inside your head and in doing so, quickly relaxes. This shift can result in three different general patterns:

- For some, going to sleep can be easier. And their sleep quality is deeper and more restorative.

- For others, they may require less sleep than they used to. This happens because the energy of consciousness is not consumed and rather, has increased. Some people only sleep for five or six hours, some even less. But they still have a good amount of energy and feel good.

- Some may experience that the Shenji and ñ practices activate their consciousness, and at night they cannot sleep well. This becomes a source of worry, so energy is consumed and they can become tired. If you experience an activation, there is no need to worry. Just realize this is qi movement. Practice Shenji and ñ more gently, or even silently, to avoid creating tension in Shenji Palace. If you find tension there, bring your consciousness down to Mingmen Inner Palace and rest there. The qi will follow and calm down. This can also help you sleep.

5. How can I feel the qi of the universe?

We do not and cannot feel universal qi with our five senses. So the practice is to use your consciousness to merge with the universe. Consciousness can be aware of it even if it is very subtle, and your consciousness can simply merge with the qi universe.

Feeling the qi of the universe is not a method — it is an ability you develop in your gongfu. If your consciousness is pure enough, you will experience the qi of the universe.

The way to come to experience the qi of the universe is to make your consciousness finer and purer. So, how can you make your consciousness purer? Observe finer and finer levels of qi. First, observe the inner space of the body at finer and finer levels, going deeper and deeper. Then observe the universe and merge with it. Do not use your physical senses to measure or analyze universal qi. Use your Pure Consciousness to observe and experience it. It is different from the senses of the body.

6. What about the Huiyin point at the perineum?

We gently lift up Huiyin to prevent energy from leaking from that point. Do not worry if you forget to do this during practice. During Throat Breathing, just focus on the breathing and do not mind Huiyin. When you practice deep Throat Breathing, the breathing will naturally lift up Huiyin.

7. Why do we only share good experiences and not negative ones?

Some have asked whether they can share negative experiences. The answer is no — we only share good experiences. If you have a negative experience — what you might label as "bad" — you need to try to change the information in your consciousness through the practices you have learned.

When you share "good" information, our collective information field becomes stronger, manifesting more information that supports life. So when others share good information, you receive that in turn, and it will quickly effect a change from a negative state to a positive one. The more you enjoy life, the more good information you have, the more beautiful your life state becomes. And the more you share good things with others, the more you create a harmonious life state.

Even if you have a lot of suffering, you can choose to focus on the good aspects of life. Let's say you have nine sources of suffering and only one source of happiness. Choose to share this one source of happiness with others — the power of this information can increase. You then enlarge and multiply your one source of happiness. It becomes two, three, four, five, six sources of happiness. When you share happiness, others receive this love and also send love back to you. This will magnify your own happiness.

Some may have only two sources of suffering and eight sources of happiness. But if they fixate on the two sources of suffering, these sources enlarge and multiply, while the sources of happiness diminish.

Our practice is to always support the positive information to bring about more balance and flow. This kind of sharing supports the whole field. Share the honey with others, but not the poison — to benefit the world, to love the world. This is the larger scope of our practice. This is a process of transformation.

Note: Sharing only "good" information doesn't mean you cannot reference any challenges you have. It means you do not fixate on the details or the information of negative thought spirals, which are from the old, conditioned reference framework.

One day, when you and your sharing circle are ready go beyond the duality of "good and bad," you can share everything. As the awakened observer, you and others can receive power and wisdom from any sharing.

8. For people with very sensitive constitutions, is it safe to merge with everyone? What about negative energies?

Trust that everything and everyone are qi. If your consciousness is pure enough, and if deep inside your consciousness you trust there is no problem, then there will be no problem.

You must also remember that you are not alone. Remember the entireties:

Your consciousness and the qi of the body are an entirety.

You and society form an entirety.

You and universal qi are an entirety.

You and the collective consciousness field are an entirety.

Always come to your pure Mingjue and to the world consciousness field and merge into the universe. The entirety state of your consciousness can harmonize with everything because it contains everything. It is big and powerful enough to create balance. That is why we always emphasize the world consciousness field. It is like an infinite ocean that can absorb and transform everything. This is the key — it is not you merging with others. It is you merging with the infinite collective field, which contains everything.

9. What does it mean experientially to surrender?

As a concept, surrender can guide you to relax more deeply inside.

True surrender as an experience is a high-level state. It means to be in the Pure Consciousness state, to be in the entirety state where consciousness merges with the qi universe. In this state, there are no attachments, no separateness, no duality, no struggle and no effort. This is total surrender. This is unconditional acceptance.

10. What does it mean to be a *complete person*?

Generally, humans are in a state of division. In the rougher, denser state of the material world, there is separation, a sense of duality.

To be a "complete person" means that your consciousness totally merges with your qi body and your life. This is a complete life — consciousness and the qi body become one. Beyond that, humans and nature are one, you and human society are one, all humans are one, and humans and the universe are one. This is a "complete human being."

11. What is the state of emptiness and how can I experience it?

If you have not experienced this state, do not hurry. It is because the physical body, the information about the concrete, material world is still very strong in your consciousness.

Simply continue to practice observing and relaxing. Relax your intention. Sometimes you can watch the blue sky. See how the blue sky is an empty space; it is simply the color blue. Then close your eyes and in your consciousness remember this blue sky is empty. It is a qi state.

Another exercise to try: scan your room. What do you see? Most people say, "I see the wall, furniture, a door, and maybe some people." But can you see the space in front of you? If you see the empty space and also see that the people in the room are also in empty space, this can begin to change your habit of always seeing the material world.

You can also train yourself to just watch empty space. After a while, close your eyes and bring that experience of space into your body. Actually, your body contains a lot of empty space and occupies empty space. Now you may be sitting somewhere, but when you leave, the space is still there. When you return and sit there, the space merges with you. So observe the space within you — it is qi. By observing closely and gradually, you will realize all the emptiness within and around you.

12. Can you talk about judgment?

Anyone who has thoughts will have judgments. Not all judgments cause blockages.

There are two kinds of judgment.

One kind is fixed or blocked. This kind of judgment causes you to have emotions and sensations in your body — anger, fear, disgust, or another strong emotion that creates a sensation in the body. This is the reason why we often say, "Do not judge." This means, "Do not have a fixed judgment." Fixed judgements cause strong, blocked, emotional feelings in the body.

Another kind of judgment is a neutral judgment—some may call this "discernment." This kind of judgment does not cause an emotional feeling. It happens in a very neutral and free state, an awakened state, or a high-level consciousness state.

Enlightened people also judge, but their internal state is peaceful.

13. When you are doing a healing on someone, can you describe your inner experience?

I just stay in Pure Consciousness state, receiving pure information from the consciousness field and giving it to the other person. In my consciousness, the other person is qi. I stay in a deep Mingjue consciousness state and merge with the other person's qi body. The qi body is in my Mingjue, and I just gently give this information: "Inside qi is open and flowing well, all blockages have already disappeared." It is very simple.

14. What if I am discouraged or losing hope that this practice can benefit me or my family?

For many, hope can be challenging to maintain. It is important, however, to trust the Self, trust this new (Zhineng Qigong) science, and trust the collective consciousness field. Also, to diligently practice the methods during your daily life. This is how change happens.

Sometimes change happens very quickly. At other times, slowly. Sometimes your life state sees dramatic improvement; other times, the old, fixed patterns emerge again, maybe even become stronger, and your state declines. Regardless of which you experience, the path is the same: continue to practice with compassion and commitment. And realize that change is always happening.

Some of you may think or say, "Sometimes it goes well, but then something happens, and I feel the suffering and become emotional again." This is normal! The old patterns and habits can take time to change. Work on life again. At that moment, hopefully you can realize that these are old patterns. "I judge, fight, lose my Mingjue state, and returned to the divided consciousness state."

The simple awareness that this is the old, conditioned pattern is already a change. At this point of awareness, try to come back to Mingjue state. If this is difficult, try repeating ň loudly and quickly, keeping your focus on the sound, each ň happening in the present moment, within your awakening consciousness — ň is awakening.

Sometimes the emotional habit is very powerful and when it combines with sensations in the body, it is stronger yet. Still, you can choose to not give up.

If you find yourself thinking, "It is a very emotional and difficult time. I don't feel I can come to Mingjue," know that this is a feeling state of short duration. You can always return to Mingjue. You must trust this. You can always come to the practice of repeating ň, and your Mingjue state can always improve more.

15. What is the difference between mindfulness and Mingjue practice?

Some have described mindfulness practices as being aware of the movements and physical experiences in the present moment, without judgment or interpretation. That is a very good practice, and it can be a prerequisite state toward the development of Mingjue, but it is not Mingjue.

If another level of mindfulness refers to Pure Consciousness knowing itself in the present moment, this level of mindfulness is the same as Mingjue. However, this is a discussion about the concepts. It is much more important to just practice and experience the reality.

Yiyuanti Theory and Mingjue Theory do not cover the topic of mindfulness. When there are too many concepts, more explanations are needed. Do not bring too many other concepts into our Mingjue or Yiyuanti practice. In Mingjue Gongfu, we simply practice the state of Pure Consciousness and let go of other thoughts.

16. What if there are conflicts with practicing Mingjue Gongfu and other practices like yoga or other methods in Zhineng Qigong like Level One or Two?

Mingjue Gongfu is for improving the power and ability of consciousness. Therefore, there is no real conflict with any other method.

However, when you practice Mingjue for a longer period of time — for example, one, two, or three hours — you likely will not have time to practice other methods. Do not worry. If your Mingjue is improved, you can use the high-level Mingjue state to practice the other methods. This will make the other methods more effective, and your experience deeper.

So I suggest that you practice Mingjue every day, then use the high-level Mingjue state to practice the movements you need and like (Level One and Level Two). When you practice the movements, keep your Mingjue stable. It is as if your whole body becomes a Mingjue body. Mingjue is always in the process of sending and receiving information. And at this level, Level One and Level Two can make your bodily qi flow well while also improving your Mingjue Gongfu.

If, during your movement practices, you lose your Mingjue in the physical feeling, do not worry. You have already come to a deeper level. Over time, you will discover your own personal way to practice, depending on your needs and preferences. You can practice Mingjue Wall Squats, Mingjue Taiji Balls, Mingjue Lift Qi Up Pour Qi Down, Mingjue Body Mind.

17. Can you speak about guilt or the guilty conscience?

Guilt arises when you want do something you feel is wrong or selfish, or you do something with an unintended consequence. Guilt can serve a useful function in society — to keep people from potentially harming others — but it also can block your life.

If you have a strong sense of guilt, you are attaching to the past and this can block your life force and energy flow. This creates a deep stress, even depression. It is like pollution. If you feel guilty, it means you do not and cannot love yourself.

If you did something wrong, then put it down. The old self made a wrong choice, but that time has already passed. Decide deep in your heart not to do this again in the future. This decision can make everything right again. There is no guilt anymore. Liberate yourself.

Enjoy and appreciate the new "you" in this present moment — a Mingjue person, a universal love person, a beautiful person. Confirm yourself, love yourself. In this present moment feel, "I am pure Mingjue." And suddenly, you can go beyond the past and be free. Haola!

18. Why are some past symptoms or health challenges returning after I started practicing Mingjue Gongfu?

If this happens to you, it means that, at the rough level, the problem had already disappeared. However, some blockages and painful or imbalanced information still exist at the subtle levels. How do you respond to this? Continue practicing Mingjue universal love into that space. The harmonious information gathers there and transforms the qi in that space. (See Mingjue Healing for more information.)

19. Can you explain how Mingjue Fasting is different than regular fasting?

Fasting is an effective way to purify and stabilize the Mingjue state.

In Mingjue Fasting, you receive this information (to fast). Then you stop eating. All others activities remain normal. It's that simple! Mingjue-level fasting is information fasting, meaning that good information will create everything you need in the fasting state. You just need to trust the information.

Another level of fasting is to practice qi — trust that qi that will nourish the body. This fasting practice is more complicated, but is also very effective. Qi-level fasting means you practice gathering universal qi into your qi body. And when you are hungry, practice gathering universal qi into your qi body some more, merging with the qi universe.

20. How do we avoid consuming too much qi with sexual activity?

- Practice Mingjue well.

- Practice the qi of Mingmen inner space and kidneys qi.

- Practice the coccyx movements, forward and backward — together with Throat Breathing. Teacher Wei's recommendation: do this 100-300 times a day!

- For those who are not sexually active, the sexual organs and Mingmen Inner Palace qi can still be made stronger.

21. For practices with specific directionality, like Right Angle Breathing or Light Healing Rotation, does it matter if we are sitting up instead of lying down?

It does not truly matter, because everything is Hun Yuan Qi. It is better to sit upright, but lying down is fine, too.

氣充足

氣血流通

功能正常

Qì Chong Zu
Qi is abundant

Qì Xue Liu Tong
Qi and blood flow well

Gong Neng Zhen Chang
Functions are perfect

CLOSING REMARKS
BY TEACHER WEI

From deep in my heart, I thank you for your diligent practice and pure intention. Your experiences support our consciousness field, information field, and qi field.

Thank you to all the organizers and participants for loving each other and supporting each other in our consciousness field.

When we reflect on the lessons of Mingjue Gongfu, it seems like we covered a lot of theories and methods. However, Mingjue works with everything — the internal world and the external one, with everything merging into a Mingjue Entirety state. So in essence, all the theories and methods are just bringing us to practice this single state. This state — the peaceful, harmonious Mingjue Entirety — is the real teacher.

It is all very simple.

Now everybody, stay in your best Mingjue state… forever!

Hun Yuan Ling Tong.

INDEX

Made in the USA
Las Vegas, NV
16 September 2024

95361105R00136